What if God?

A Personal Devotion / Bible Study

MITCH WOODARD

Copyright © 2016 Mitch Woodard.

All rights reserved. No part of this book may be used or reproduced by any means, graphic, electronic, or mechanical, including photocopying, recording, taping or by any information storage retrieval system without the written permission of the author except in the case of brief quotations embodied in critical articles and reviews.

Scriptures taken from the Holy Bible, New International Version®, NIV®. Copyright © 1973, 1978, 1984, 2011 by Biblica, Inc.™ Used by permission of Zondervan. All rights reserved worldwide. www.zondervan.com The "NIV" and "New International Version" are trademarks registered in the United States Patent and Trademark Office by Biblica, Inc.™ All rights reserved.

Scripture taken from the King James Version of the Bible.

This book is a work of non-fiction. Unless otherwise noted, the author and the publisher make no explicit guarantees as to the accuracy of the information contained in this book and in some cases, names of people and places have been altered to protect their privacy.

WestBow Press books may be ordered through booksellers or by contacting:

WestBow Press
A Division of Thomas Nelson & Zondervan
1663 Liberty Drive
Bloomington, IN 47403
www.westbowpress.com
1 (866) 928-1240

Because of the dynamic nature of the Internet, any web addresses or links contained in this book may have changed since publication and may no longer be valid. The views expressed in this work are solely those of the author and do not necessarily reflect the views of the publisher, and the publisher hereby disclaims any responsibility for them.

Any people depicted in stock imagery provided by Thinkstock are models, and such images are being used for illustrative purposes only.

Certain stock imagery © Thinkstock.

ISBN: 978-1-5127-4474-3 (sc)
ISBN: 978-1-5127-4475-0 (hc)
ISBN: 978-1-5127-4473-6 (e)

Library of Congress Control Number: 2016909116

Print information available on the last page.

WestBow Press rev. date: 8/23/2016

PREFACE

In a culture where everything connected with Christianity seems to be under fire and the encroachment of worldliness can cause the very foundations of our faith to be compromised, *What If God?* will help us anchor our faith and cause us to develop a deeper relationship with our Savior.

What If God? is a devotional guide that contains twelve chapters, one for each month of the year, and fifty-two subjects, one for each week of the year. Begin each devotion on the first day of each week by simply reading the narrative as it is written, without necessarily using the provided study guide and references the first day. Carefully read the devotion and ruminate on its contents.

On the second day, use the provided study guide and references to add the weight of God's Word to the content, noting the areas of the devotion and the scriptures most meaningful to you. My hope is that you will be prompted to read the scriptures in context while contemplating the concepts I mention and draw applicable truths and promises from both. If you are just beginning your walk with the Lord, this part of the exercise may take most of the week. If, on the other hand, you are well-grounded in the Word, may you be encouraged by the application.

I have provided a study guide and worksheet with applicable scripture references, a "Point of Truth," and a question for "Practical Application" to your personal life. You will notice there is one paragraph in each devotion that is the author's reflection on the subject. These reflections all begin with "Consider" and are not included in the study guide or reference sheet but are for you to "consider". As you spend time each week, my prayer is that you will ponder the truths of the application and think of ways to practically apply them to your life. Note the application if that is helpful. In all likelihood, some applications will require more work than others, but my hope is that you will begin to think of God in a much larger sense than you may currently think of Him, for He is much more than we can truly comprehend.

If you are using *What If God?* in a small group setting or Bible study, study one narrative of the chapter each week. Two weeks may be required if the study is a typical hour and you purpose to go in depth. If you are the study leader, ask each participant to prepare beforehand and bring a completed reference worksheet to the study for discussion and interaction. The study leader should keep the discussion on topic and take the group members as deeply into God's Word as they may endeavor to go concerning the subject matter in the narrative.

Each devotion/small group Bible study begins with a question that will hopefully lead you to a thought-provoking search with the subject at hand. Many of the truths are hidden in questions, but using questions leaves room to enter into matters that have been debated over the centuries. While some of these issues are controversial, they are hopefully not offensive, as many truths are put forth for you to consider the scriptural applications as they connect with particular truths. Hopefully this will cause you to reflect, above all else, on the greatness and wonders of our majestic God.

My prayer is that *What If God?* will bring you to a place where you are willing to believe God's Word even in difficult times when God's Word doesn't always seem to make sense. Above all else, however, may you dig deep into His Word to know God in all His fullness and not be swayed by wrong doctrine and men with persuasive words. Instead, may you become well grounded in Him and His wonders throughout His Word.

2 Timothy 3:16-17 of the Interlinear Bible says:

Every Scripture is God-breathed and is profitable for teaching, for reproof, for correction, for instruction in righteousness; so that the man of God may be perfect, fully furnished for every good work.

And Hebrews 4:12-13 of the Interlinear Bible says:

For the word of God is living and powerfully working and sharper than every two-edged sword, even piercing as far as the dividing apart of both soul and spirit, of both joints and marrow, and able to judge of the thoughts and intentions of the heart; and there is no creature unrevealed before Him; but all things are naked and laid open to His eyes, with whom is our account.

If, as you are reading *What if God?*, you begin to question whether you are a true believer in Jesus or whether you've ever received Jesus as your Savior, remember — being saved is so simple a child can do it. It is the working out of that salvation and obedience to Jesus' commands that is the true evidence you are His child and have been regenerated by His Holy Spirit. This regeneration is a concealed work of God and is only revealed by the mentioned evidence of obedience. Remember God's man, David, was an adulterer, murderer, and disobedient in so many ways, but when God, through His prophet Nathan, revealed David's sin in one particular instance, he humbled himself and repented of that sin and God always forgave his sincere repentance in every situation.

The following scriptures are called the "Romans Road" to salvation because they explain clearly how to be saved from God's coming wrath and become part of the servants of God.

1. Romans 3:23: "for all have sinned and fall short of the glory of God."

2. Romans 6:23: "For the wages of sin is death, but the gift of God is eternal life in Jesus Christ our Lord."

3. Romans 5:8: "But God demonstrates his own love for us in this: While we were still sinners, Christ died for us."

4. Romans 10:9: "That if you confess with your mouth, 'Jesus is Lord,' and believe in your heart that God raised Jesus from the dead, you will be saved."

5. Romans 10:13: "for, everyone who calls on the name of the Lord will be saved."

If you have read God's Word or heard His voice in it, and, as a result, you are drawn to Him, realizing you are a sinner in need of forgiveness, He will lead you down the Romans Road and pray to Him according to its instructions. Your prayer may sound something like this:

Jesus, I know I am a sinner and I want to receive your gift of eternal life. I am grateful that you died for me and I speak right now that you are Lord, Jesus, and I believe the Father God raised you from the dead. I call on your name and you tell me now that I am saved. Thank you, Jesus.

Becoming a servant of God is that simple, and I pray you have made this decision. If you have, God is in you already, for you have been indwelt with His Holy Spirit and your heart has been made new. You are now, therefore, a dwelling place of God. He resides within you, and, as you mature, walk out your faith believing God is who His Word portrays Him to be. He will ensure you are molded into a vessel of His mercy and will be used for His purposes.

I pray that *What if God?* will serve as a repeated benefit as you mature as a believer in Jesus Christ.

CONTENTS

Chapter One: Unique Attributes of God 1
1. God's Omniscience 1
2. God's Omnipresence 6
3. God's Omnipotence 11
4. God's Immutability 15
5. God's Sovereignty 20

Chapter Two: Prayer 25
6. Prayer 25
7. Pray Always 30
8. Praying and Fasting 35

Chapter Three: Worship and Giving 39
9. Praise and Worship 39
10. Adoration 43
11. Giving 46
12. Possessions 51
13. Treasure 54

Chapter Four: Trials and Interaction with Others 58
14. Trials 58
15. Voice of the Shepherd / Witnessing 62
16. Relationships 67
17. Forgiveness 70
18. Anxieties 74

Chapter Five: Discernment 78
19. Making Wise Judgments 78
20. Truth, Love, and Judgment 83
21. Truth, Love, and Compassion 87

Chapter Six: Old Covenant Application to Contemporary Life 92
22. Diet 92
23. God's Power 97
24. God's Intervention 102
25. God's Mercy 106
26. Trusting God 111
27. Standing Alone 116

Chapter Seven: Person and Work of Jesus 121
28. Jesus 121
29. Sin's Defeat 127
30. Jewish Feast / Jesus 132
31. Sign of Jonah 137
32. Parables 142
33. Contemporary Pharisees 147

Chapter Eight: Christian Life / Man's Responsibility 152
34. Believer's Freedom 152
35. Believer's Privilege 157
36. God's Bride 162
37. True Believers 167
38. Love the Lord 173

Chapter Nine: Christian Life / God's Sovereignty 179

39. Righteousness 179
40. God's Field / Sanctification 184
41. Idolatry 189
42. Is He Lord? 194
43. Holiness 199

Chapter Ten: Family 204

44. God's Protocol 204
45. Husbands and Wives 209
46. Families / Kingdom of Heaven 214
47. Prodigal 219

Chapter Eleven: Angels and Heaven 224

48. Angels 224
49. Going Home 230

Chapter Twelve: A Sovereign God 235

50. God's Ownership 235
51. God's Sovereign Choice 240
52. All Israel Will Be Saved 246

CHAPTER ONE
UNIQUE ATTRIBUTES OF GOD

I.   God's Omniscience

What if God is really all-knowing from the beginning to infinity? With such an infinite attribute, we may begin to understand why He is never caught off guard or surprised by the events on earth. God being mindful of every event that has and is to take place, from the smallest detail, to the vastness of His creation that glorifies its Creator. He would know every decision that every individual has or will make, the cause that influenced each decision, and every antecedent involved in it, for all time. This omniscient God would also know the effects and outcomes of all those decisions. He would foreknow every tear that would be shed. He gives every hair that would ever be on every head a number.

Consider the busiest time of day on a New York City afternoon, every pedestrian, every car and taxi, driver and passenger. This omniscient God knows every thought and inclination, reason and purpose that motivates or depresses each living soul in the crowded scene in your mind. Consider each and every creature seen and unseen, in the air or under foot, and in the ground under the tons of concrete and asphalt. He knows the purpose He ordained for all those creatures to perform. And while God has perfect knowledge of this New York City scene, the same can be said for every place on earth and in the heavens.

He also knows the hearts of all those that would be, from the first man He created from dust, and all those who were born after. And an even more mysterious truth, concerning many of those hearts, is how He would enable or grant the ability and grace for them to turn in repentance to Him. It seems with omniscience, He always knew His creation would be deceived and fall from their created position. And in so doing blood would have to be spilled -His blood- to atone for the sins that would follow.

All-knowing wise God, thank You that Your knowledge and wisdom are above all and You have given us a glimpse of Yourself in your Word.

Chapter One
Unique Attributes of God

I. God's Omniscience/Study Guide

What if God is really all knowing...

1. from the beginning to infinity? (Isaiah 40:13-14; I Corinthians 2:16; Job 21:22 & 37:16)

2. With such an infinite attribute, we may begin to understand why He is never caught off guard or surprised by events on earth. God is mindful of every event that has and is to take place, from the smallest detail, to the vastness of His creation that glorifies its Creator. He would know every decision that every individual has made or will make, the cause that influenced each decision, and every antecedent involved in it, for all time. This omniscient God would also know the effects and outcomes of all those decisions. He would foreknow every tear that would be shed. (Psalm 56:8)

3. He gives every hair that would ever be on every head a number. (Matthew 10:30)

4. He knows the hearts of all those who would be, from the first man He created from the dust, and all those who were born after. (Jeremiah 17:9-10 & I Samuel 16:7)

5. He also knows which of those hearts He would enable or grant (John 6:65)

6. the ability and grace to turn to Him in repentance because He has always known His creation would be deceived and fall from its created position. (Genesis 3:1-7)

7. And in so doing, blood would have to be spilled – His blood – to atone for the sins that would follow. (Romans 3:25)

All-knowing wise God, thank You that Your knowledge and wisdom are above all, and You have given us a glimpse of Yourself in your Word.

References for God's Omniscience

1. Isaiah 40:13-14

   I Corinthians 2:16

   Job 21:22

   Job 37:16

2. Psalm 56:8

3. Matthew 10:30

4. Jeremiah 17:9-10

   I Samuel 16:7

5. John 6:65

6. Genesis 3:1-7

7. Romans 3:25

Point of Truth: God knows every detail, act, and thought of all His creation, past, present, and future.

Practical Application: How does God's omniscience affect your life and your perception of Him?

2. God's Omnipresence

What if God is really everywhere at once from the depths to the heights from east to west? With such a presence we not only may find ourselves more aware of our character when we are alone but we find comfort in never really being alone. Would that mean that this God transcends time and that is part of why He said He is the Alpha and Omega? He is past, present, and future all the time. He is eternally I Am. Maybe in those exceptionally difficult times we can be reminded He is there and our 'Abba Father' is as close as we are willing to draw near to Him. His very Spirit indwells the soul of every regenerated believer all at the same time.

Consider that the eternal God was never created, He is. And when we speak of God we actually are speaking of the trinity, God the Father, God the Son (Jesus) and God the Holy Spirit all uncreated and perfect in every way. Now think of today's world with the busyness of everyday life and many different enticing ways offered to have a relationship with god. But all these deities and their prophets have lived and died and are no more. Oh, except One. The triune God and His begotten incarnate Son, Jesus Christ. Yes, He died but He still Is, as His presence never died, only His incarnate body and that body supernaturally came back to life and in doing so forever established Himself as I Am, Eternal forever and ever. And He is the only true God and He must be recognized as so.

Also a great reminder of His omnipresence is the Jewish Feast of Booths where the Jews celebrate their time of wandering in the desert when they lived in booths. Part of the celebration is to use four plant species, three different species of branches bound together and an etrog (variation of a lemon). Branches in one hand and the etrog in the other, the Jews then wave the branches in every direction, north, south, east, and west to acknowledge the omnipresence of God. And this just happens to be the only festival that will continue to be celebrated in the millennial kingdom with some strong implications spoken of, if nations refuse to participate in this festival. Might that speak to just how depraved man is when he refuses Jesus' invitation when He is the eternal King living among us on earth. Sound familiar? What a comfort to know He is with us, always.

Eternal God, help us to see You in all majesty and glory and that Your presence is in all that is.

2. God's Omnipresence/Study Guide

What if God...

1. is really everywhere... (Proverbs 15:3)

2. At once from the depths to the heights, from the east to the west? (Psalm 139:7-10)

3. With such a presence, we not only may find ourselves more aware of our character when we are alone, but we also find comfort in never really being alone. Would that mean this God transcends time, which is part of why He said He is the Alpha and the Omega? (Revelation 1:8)

4. He is past, present, and future all the time. He is eternally I Am. (Exodus 3:14)

5. Maybe in exceptionally difficult times, we can be reminded that He, our "Abba Father," is as close as we are willing to draw near to Him. (James 4:8)

6. His very Spirit indwells the soul of every regenerated believer at the same time. Also the Jewish Feast of Booths, where the Jews celebrate their time of wandering in the desert when they lived in booths, is a great reminder of God's omnipresence. Part of the celebration entailed using four plant species: three different species of branches bound together and an etrog (variation of a lemon). The Israelites held the branches in one hand and the etrog in the other. They then waved the branches in every direction: north, south, east, and west to acknowledge the omnipresence of God. (Leviticus 23:33-43 See www.jewfaq.org /sukkot) .

7. And this just happens to be the only festival that will continue to be celebrated in the millennial kingdom with some strong implications

spoken of, if nations refuse to participate in this festival. (Zechariah 14:16-19)

8. Might that speak to just how depraved man is when he refuses Jesus' invitation when He is the eternal King living among us on earth. Sound familiar? What a comfort to know He is with us, always. (Matthew 28:20)

Eternal God, help us see You in all majesty and glory and Your presence in all that is.

References for God's Omnipresence

1. Proverbs 15:3

2. Psalm 139:7-10

3. Revelation 1:8

4. Exodus 3:14

5. James 4:8

6. Leviticus 23:33-43

7. Matthew 28:20

Point of Truth: God is I AM always. He transcends time and is eternal: past, present, and future. He is always everywhere.

Practical Application: How does God's omnipresence affect your life and your perception of Him?

3. God's Omnipotence

What if God is really all-powerful and does control every event in the universe and possibly beyond? And that causes us to ponder the terrible tragedies like earthquakes, tsunamis, floods, droughts, acts of war, terrorism and violence of all kinds and while pondering realize there is a weaker but very strong unseen force that up to this point has legal control over the hearts of all those who are not believers. The same event that gave him legal control also caused all of nature to go from perfection to varying degrees of chaos. Now we need cautiously to remember that all of these events are still allowed by a Sovereign God to whom that weaker power is still completely subject. With that in mind, maybe at our weaker moments, might we resist the temptation to blame Him for the violence and destruction on earth and then know where it truly originates?

Consider the power that was required to send the space shuttles into space, accomplish whatever purposes were determined, and bring them back safely. Or the scenes you have viewed of an atomic explosion and realize that it is God that has granted the wisdom to achieve such feats of power. God created the sun with a seemingly inexhaustible source of energy and the entire universe with myriads of stars and the power required for them to be seen. And this omnipotent God created all these elements by the power of His spoken word.

Also we might find encouragement knowing that when Jesus was crucified and then by the power of this omnipotent God, life returned to a lifeless body. By that same power, a fulfillment of a specific prophecy began the, seemingly slow, but certain demise of that lesser power. With that the church age began and His intention for the church is not only to bring the full number of Gentiles in, but also to show the many different elements of the wisdom of God by making known to the rulers and authorities in the heavenly realms His eternal purpose which He accomplished in Jesus! Satan's destruction is as sure as God is sovereign! Even so come quickly Lord Jesus!

Omnipotent God, give us the grace to walk daily in Your power and resist the power and temptation the enemy of our souls would offer.

3. God's Omnipotence/Study Guide

What if God...

1. is really all powerful and controls every event in the universe and possibly beyond? (Hebrews 1:3-4)

2. And that causes us to ponder the terrible tragedies like earthquakes, tsunamis, floods, droughts, acts of war, terrorism, and violence of all kinds, while realizing there is a weaker, but very strong, unseen force that up to this point has legal control over the hearts of all those who are not believers. (Matthew 24:4-14 & John 8:44)

3. The same event that gave that force legal control also caused all of nature to go from perfection to varying degrees of chaos. (Genesis 3:1-7)

4. Now we need to remember cautiously that a Sovereign God, to whom that weaker power is still completely subject, still allows all these events. (Job 1:12)

5. With that, maybe at our weaker moments, might we resist the temptation to blame God for the violence and destruction on earth and know where it truly comes from. We might also find encouragement in knowing that when Jesus was crucified, by the power of this omnipotent God, life returned to His lifeless body. (1 Corinthians 6:14)

6. By that same power, a fulfillment of a specific prophecy... (Genesis 3:15)

7. began the seemingly slow... (2 Peter 3:8)

8. but certain demise of that lesser power. With that, the church age began and His intention for the church is not only to bring the full number of Gentiles in... (Romans 11:25)

9. but also to show the many different elements of the wisdom of God by making known to the rulers and authorities in the heavenly realm His eternal purpose, which He accomplished in Jesus! (Ephesians 3:10-11)

10. Satan's destruction is as sure as God is sovereign! Even so, come quickly, Lord Jesus! (Revelation 20:7-10)

Omnipotent God, give us the grace to walk daily in Your power and resist the power and temptation the enemy of our souls would offer.

References for God's Omnipotence

1. Hebrews 1:3-4

2. Matthew 24:4-14

    John 8:44

3. Genesis 3:1-7

4. Job 1:12

5. 1 Corinthians 6:14

6. Genesis 3:15

7. 2 Peter 3:8

8. Romans 11:25

9. Ephesians 3:10-11

10. Revelation 20:7-10

Point of Truth: God is the one all-powerful being, and all things are subject to His power. Nothing happens without Him allowing it to happen, and He uses good and evil events and individuals to accomplish His purposes and will.

Practical Application: How does God's omnipotence affect your life and your perception of Him?

4. God's Immutability

What if God cannot lie and never changes and is so beyond our way of thinking that He would initiate a conversation with two of His chosen servants for a specific purpose? As Moses was in God's presence receiving the Ten Commandments written by God's hand, God informs Moses that the people he is leading have engaged in vile idolatry and because of such wickedness God says that He is angered to the point that He will destroy this people, then pauses. Moses intercedes for the people and God stays His destruction of all the people and delays it for some.

In a similar situation with Abraham, God again initiates the conversation and informs Abraham of His plans to destroy Sodom. Then He confirmed His blessing on Abraham, after which those with the Lord turned away to go toward Sodom but the Lord knew what Abraham was going to do. What appears to be a man dealing with God in no way was. The Lord was allowing Abraham to know Him better as a God full of mercy, but also full of wrath on the wicked. God also taught Abraham, Moses and us to show mercy and to intercede.

Consider what it means when God himself states that He does not change. But scripture seems to imply that at times, such as mentioned, He did change. But He doesn't, so we are compelled to look deeper to see what we might find. Think that when we have an emotion, that is what we are feeling. Maybe the emotion is anger or happiness or excitement. Then think that when God displays an emotion, it is always, just as He is always I AM. God is always full of mercy and compassion toward those who are truly repentant and always full of anger and wrath toward the unrepentant. He is always, everything that He is, without changing. Yes, it is difficult to grasp, but that is who God is, He doesn't get mad and explode in anger after He has had enough. He simply displays His emotions, which are always present and controlled, as He has determined when and how He will display the emotion.

God's ways and thoughts are so beyond ours as He patiently and purposely is molding Moses to be the merciful, compassionate leader of an obstinate people. This was one step in that process. He was preparing Abraham, on the other hand, to trust Him explicitly for the test he would soon endure with the apparent sacrifice of his son Isaac. God never changed and cannot do so, but as a loving Father speaking to His admiring sons, He allowed Moses and Abraham to become more conformed to His image with their intercession. Might that also cause us to search more diligently to understand the attributes of such a mysterious and majestic God?

Unchanging God, enable us accept You as You are presented in Your Word.

4. God's Immutability/Study Guide

What if God...

1. cannot lie and never changes... (I Samuel 15:29, Numbers 23:19, & Malachi 3:6)

2. and is so beyond our way of thinking that He would initiate a conversation with two of His chosen servants for a specific purpose? As Moses received the Ten Commandments God wrote with His own hand, while in His very presence, God informs Moses the people he is leading have engaged in vile idolatry. Because of such wickedness God says He is angered to the point that He will destroy this people, then pauses. Moses intercedes for the people, and God stays His destruction of all the people and delays it for some. (Exodus 32:7-14)

3. Similarly, with Abraham, God initiates a conversation with him and informs Abraham that He plans to destroy Sodom. Then He confirms His blessing on Abraham, after which those with the Lord turn away to go toward Sodom, but the Lord knew what Abraham was going to do. (Genesis 18:16-33)

4. What appears to be a man dealing with God in no way was. The Lord was allowing Abraham to know Him better as a God full of mercy... (James 5:11)

5. but also full of wrath on the wicked. (Romans 1:18-19)

6. God also taught Abraham, Moses, and us to show mercy... (Jude 1:22-23)

7. and to intercede. (Ephesians 6:18; I Thessalonians 5:25)

8. God's ways and thoughts are so beyond ours... (Isaiah 55:8-9)

9. as He patiently and purposely molded Moses to be the merciful, compassionate, leader of an obstinate people. This was one step in that process. He was preparing Abraham, on the other hand, to trust Him explicitly for the test he would soon endure with the apparent sacrifice of his son, Isaac. God never changed and cannot do so, but as a loving Father speaking to His admiring sons, He allowed Moses and Abraham to become more conformed to His image with their intercession. Might that also cause us to search more diligently to understand the attributes of such a mysterious and majestic God? (Romans 8:29 & I Corinthians 3:18)

Unchanging God, enable us accept You as You present yourself in Your Word.

References for God's Immutability

1. I Samuel 15:29

   Numbers 23:19

   Malachi 3:6

2. Exodus 32:7-14

3. Genesis 18:16-33

4. James 5:11

5. Romans 1:18-19

6. Jude 1:22-23

7. I Thessalonians 5:25

   Ephesians 6:18

8. Isaiah 55:8-9

9. Romans 8:29

   I Corinthians 3:18

Point of Truth: God does not and will never change. He cannot change or lie. If He could change, we could not trust Him.

Practical Application: How does God's immutability affect your life and your perception of him?

5. God's Sovereignty

What if God in His unique attributes of omniscience, omnipresence, omnipotence and immutability (unchanging) knows that in our frailty we would sometimes doubt and question Him? Might we also consider one other attribute that is uniquely God in that He is holy, which would complete what has been revealed as to His sovereignty? * His holiness is different than the other mentioned attributes as it is present in all His attributes. Can you image an omnipotent being without holiness? But in the marvelous work of salvation He imputes His holiness to His children and in Jesus' atoning blood we stand as holy, seated with Christ as His bride. This is a mystery within itself but what a wonderful position we have been blessed to have.

But back to His sovereignty, might these unique attributes be what make Him Sovereign over all else? As God does, we also can show the attributes of mercy, love, grace, kindness, honesty, goodness, patience and the list could go on. So with the five unique attributes that make God sovereign, might we always let those truths be the foundation when we study His word? Especially in difficult areas where it might appear God changed His mind or regretted acting and would have preferred to do something differently? And what about places that seem to be contradictory?

Consider just what sovereignty means; that God answers to no one, and He owes no one in any measure. He has purposely made Himself mysterious and sometimes even distant, seemingly. But think about it, He is God and reserves for Himself to act as He chooses. But we can be assured of His perfections in all that He is and does. This does not mean we can understand or figure, with our limited logic, all that exists in the Almighty. We can be grateful He has gifted us with a glimpse of His being in His word and gladly accept Him as He is presented as perfect and trustworthy. Or the alternative is an option, but a risky one, to recreate Him as we would like Him to be.

Might we trust Him no matter what, as Abraham learned and walked in His belief of God, to be confident that He is faithful and can be trusted even if He says He is going to require something of us that appears to be the very practice He says He hates so much? Being mindful of such a difficult test, might we be encouraged to place our belief and trust in Him even when what He says does not seem logical to our simple minds or maybe we just don't like some of the difficult truths of His word.

Sovereign Lord, grant us the grace to walk in Your ways, to believe and trust You no matter what, knowing You are trustworthy and faithful, as we strive to be obedient, believing that You are perfect in all Your ways!

* Note: God's elect angels (1Timothy 5:21) may also be considered holy, but not perfect as is God, since their purposes can be frustrated as ours can by the enemy as in Daniel10:12-13.

5. God's Sovereignty/Study Guide

What if God...

1. in His unique attributes of omniscience, omnipresence, omnipotence, and immutability (unchanging), knows that in our frailty we would sometimes doubt and question Him? Might we also consider one other attribute that is uniquely God in that He is holy... (Revelation 4:8)

2. which would complete what has been revealed as to His sovereignty? * His holiness is different from the other mentioned attributes as it is present in all His attributes. Can you image an omnipotent being without holiness? But in the marvelous work of salvation, He imputes His holiness to His children and in Jesus' atoning blood we stand as holy, seated with Christ as His bride. (Ephesians 1:4 & 2:6-7)

3. This is a mystery within itself but what a wonderful position we have been blessed to have. (Ephesians 5:32)

4. But back to His sovereignty, might these unique attributes be what make Him Sovereign over all else? As God does, we also can show the attributes of mercy, love, grace, kindness, honesty, goodness, patience and the list could go on. (2 Peter 1:5-9)

5. So with the five unique attributes that make God sovereign, might we always let those truths be the foundation when we study His Word? Especially in difficult areas where it might appear God changed His mind or regretted acting and would have preferred to do something differently. And what about places that seem to be contradictory? Might we trust Him no matter what, as Abraham learned and walked in His belief of God... (Romans 4:3 & Galatians 3:6)

6. to be confident that He is faithful and can be trusted even if He says He is going to require something of us... (Genesis 22:2)

7. that appears to be the very practice He says he hates so much? (Deuteronomy 18:9-13)

8. Being mindful of such a difficult test, might we be encouraged to place our belief and trust in Him even when what He says does not seem logical to our simple minds... (Deuteronomy 29:29 & Psalms 111:7)

9. or maybe we just don't like some of the difficult truths of His Word. (Deuteronomy 32:4)

Sovereign Lord, grant us the grace to walk in Your ways, to believe and trust You no matter what, knowing You are trustworthy and faithful as we strive to be obedient, believing that You are perfect in all Your ways!

* Note: God's elect angels (1 Timothy 5:21) may also be considered holy, but not perfect as is God, since their purposes can be frustrated as ours can by the enemy as in Daniel 10:12-13.

References for God's Sovereignty

1. Revelation 4:8

2. Ephesians 1:4

    Ephesians 2:6-7

3. Ephesians 5:32

4. 2 Peter 1:5-9

5. Romans 4:3

    Galatians 3:6

6. Genesis 22:2

7. Deuteronomy 18:9-13

8. Deuteronomy 29:29

    Psalm 111:7

9. Deuteronomy 32:4

Point of Truth: God is sovereign over all His creation and nothing happens without Him willing or allowing it. He is perfect and cannot make mistakes!

Practical Application: How does God's sovereignty affect your life and your perception of Him?

CHAPTER TWO

PRAYER

6. Prayer

What if God really knows our needs before we ask, but in His wisdom tells us to make our petitions and pleas known to Him in prayer? In doing so, we not only may realize the benefit of spending time in conversation with the One who knows us better than we know ourselves. He also reminds us to pray secretly, which may ensure that we are praying not to be seen of men but with pure motives not using many useless words that we may be tempted to be prideful of. With that practice, our public prayers might also be from pure motives.

This may also give us insight and understanding into how important it is to forgive others even when it is a most difficult task to do! God reminds us that He does not hear the prayer of a man that regards sin in his heart. With that, we will hopefully be motivated to spend more time in His Word offering our bodies as living sacrifices, which is pleasing to Him. As a result, our minds will be transformed as we learn more of Him concerning all the matters in our lives.

Consider what comes to mind when you think of praying, is it going through a check list of wants and desires, or maybe something that is formal and has to be done using certain words and patterns of speech? In reality prayer is no different than any conversation one might have with someone whom we have a relationship. However, I do not want to put God in the category of just someone, as to even begin this relationship we must be His son or daughter. With that in mind we are talking about God, the Sovereign creator of all things, who demands reverence and fear. But He is also our Father, even Abba, or Daddy. With these two aspects of His being in mind we must approach Him in humility, but boldly, realizing the work done by Him to adopt us into His family is a work that He has stated is complete.

Might this be part of understanding why He tells us He is working out all things for our good and that is only for those He foreknew and predestined to be conformed to the image of His son-His children? In addition, we are reminded He is refining the dross from our lives as we prayerfully wait on the One who says when He acts it will be quickly. As we understand the purpose for prayer seems to be more for changing us, since God doesn't change, might our prayer always be with praise on our lips, confident that His will is best and will be done as we leave our burdens with Him where we find peace that is beyond understanding.

Holy Father full of mercy, give us the grace to pray according to Your will.

Chapter Two
Prayer

6. Prayer/Study Guide

What if God…

1. really knows our needs before we ask, but in His wisdom tells us to make our petitions and pleas known to Him in prayer? (Matthew 6:8)

2. In doing so, we may realize the benefit of spending time in conversation with the One who knows us better than we know ourselves. (Matthew 10:30 & Hebrews 4:12-13)

3. He also reminds us to pray secretly, which may ensure that we are praying not to be seen of men but with pure motives not using many useless words that we may be tempted to be prideful of. With that practice, our public prayers might also be from pure motives. This may also give us insight and understanding into how important it is to forgive others even when it is a most difficult task to do! (Matthew 6:5-15)

4. God also reminds us that He does not hear the prayer of a man who regards sin in his heart. (Psalm 66:18 & Isaiah 59:1-2)

5. With that, we will hopefully be motivated to spend more time in His Word offering our bodies as living sacrifices, which is pleasing to Him. As a result, our minds will be transformed as we learn more of His will concerning all matters in our lives. (Romans 12:1-2)

6. Might this be part of our understanding why He tells us He is working out all things for the good of those He foreknew and

predestined to be conformed to the image of His son — His children? (Romans 8:28-29)

7. In addition, we are reminded that He is also refining the dross from our lives... (Proverbs 25:4)

8. as we prayerfully wait on the One who says when He acts it will be quickly. (Luke 18:1-8)

9. As we understand the purpose of prayer seems to be more for changing us, since God doesn't change, might our prayer always be with praise on our lips, confident that His will is best and will be done as we leave our burdens with Him, where we find peace that is beyond understanding? (Philippians 4:6-7)

Holy Father full of mercy, give us the grace to pray according to Your will.

References for Prayer

1. Matthew 6:8

2. Matthew 10:30

    Hebrews 4:12-13

3. Matthew 6:5-15

4. Psalm 66:18

    Isaiah 59:1-2

5. Romans 12:1-2

6. Romans 8:28-29

7. Proverbs 25:4

8. Luke 18:1-8

9. Philippians 4:6-7

Point of Truth: Prayer is God's prescribed way of relationship with His children.

Practical Application: How can my relationship with God be enhanced by speaking (praying) with Him and meditating on His Word?

7. Pray Always

What if God is so wise that He tells us to pray always, knowing that those who try to obey may realize to do such a thing, our thoughts would begin to go first to Him in every event? Is it possible, since it is not realistic for any of us to pray 24/7 in reality praying without ceasing simply means not to ever stop praying about any and everything in your life? Walking out of this command would involve our own personality and how we naturally communicate. Are we talkative, thoughtful, introverted or extraverted?

Consider the word used in the text to pray without ceasing is in relationship to a hacking cough that lingers after a cold; it seems to never cease. That is how our relationship and conversation with the Father should be as we go about our day to day lives. This also lends to the fact that we are completely dependent on Him, even for our breath, whether we realize it or not. We should always be thinking, speaking with, or listening (ruminating on His word) as our faith and trust in Christ develops. If we begin to make this our lifestyle, even when we are focusing on work, projects or relationships with others, the Father is always present in our thoughts and this will positively affect all aspects of our life.

As we communicate with our Holy Redeemer, His Spirit that dwells within might gently remind of transgressions, whether we believe they are simple or complicated, so we can repent of them and God can restore communication or dialogue between us and Him. That would mean we would need to listen, which might be a little more important than what we have to say. So just how would I go about listening to the One that apparently doesn't speak so that I can hear Him with my ears? We certainly do not want God to accuse us of having ears they did not hear, as He said so often of the Israelites and their leaders. So might that mean we need spiritual ears as God is spirit and that He speaks through his Word as we genuinely seek Him and His will in that same Word. Also His spirit may gently prompt us, but that will never contradict His Word! Might that teach us to avoid one who says "God told me" this and that, without the authority of His Word as a foundation? As praying without ceasing becomes a lifestyle, we may find ourselves increasing in admiration for the One with whom we are spending so much time communicating. The result is that we always become more like the one which we admire.

Father, enable us to always think of You first in every event You allow in our life.

7. Pray Always/Study Guide

What if God...

1. is so wise that He tells us to pray always... (I Thessalonians 5:17)

2. knowing that those who try to obey may realize if we were to do such a thing, our thoughts would begin to go first to Him in every event? Is it possible, since it is not realistic for any of us to pray 24/7 in reality that praying without ceasing simply means not to ever stop praying about any and everything in your life? Walking out this command would involve our own personality and the way we naturally communicate. Are we talkative, thoughtful, introverted, or extroverted? As we communicate with our Holy Redeemer... (Revelation 4:8 & Psalm 99:5)

3. His Spirit that dwells within us might gently remind us of our transgressions, whether we believe they are simple or complicated, so that we can repent of them and God can restore the communication or dialogue between us and Him. (Psalm 66:18)

4. That would mean we need to listen, which might be a little more important than what we have to say. So just how would I go about listening to the One who apparently doesn't speak so that I can hear Him with my ears? We certainly do not want God to accuse us of having ears that did not hear... (Isaiah 48:8 & Mark 8:17-19)

5. as He said so often of the Israelites and their leaders. So might that mean we need spiritual ears because God is a spirit and He speaks through His Word as we genuinely seek Him and His will in that same Word? Also, His spirit may gently prompt us, but that will never contradict His Word! Might that teach us to avoid one who says "God told me" this and that, without the authority of His Word as a foundation? As praying without ceasing becomes a lifestyle, we may find ourselves increasing in admiration for the

One with whom we are spending so much time communicating. The result is that we always become more like the one we admire. (Romans 8:29 & 12:2)

Father, enable us to always think of You first in every event You allow in our lives.

References for Praying Always

1. I Thessalonians 5:17

2. Revelation 4:8

   Psalm 99:5

3. Psalm 66:18

4. Isaiah 48:8

   Mark 8:17-19

5. Romans 8:29

   Romans 12:2

Point of Truth: God commands us to pray continually.

Practical Application: How can I be more consistent in praying always?

8. Praying and Fasting

What if God in His infinite wisdom would tell us that when we encounter a most unusual and difficult situation that there are times when praying and fasting are necessary to resolve the event? Not to mention that He also uses that particular prescription to cast out the most difficult "demons". So what does a demon look like or sound like or how do I even begin to know what this might mean. Well the fasting wouldn't seem to do God any good… and praying certainly allows us to speak to our Father about our concerns and needs and it is certainly how I can let my Father know how grateful I am for ALL He has and is doing for me, but that's all that's about me! But then I'm reminded of the needs of my family and friends. Oh, and God tells me to pray for workers to harvest souls, and that other brothers and sisters may be enriched in all their speaking and all their knowledge. Might my Father know that if I discipline my eating habits (fasting) I might also find other areas more disciplined? I also may realize fasting touches areas of my life other than eating, as I see what a true fast to the Father is.

Consider that true fasting as described in the text in Isaiah, speaks of caring for the needy such as widows and orphans and those who are bound, we are to set free, to clothe the one who is in need of clothes and feed those who need food. That sounds like sharing the gospel and further obeying Jesus' commands when He spoke of giving water to the thirsty is like giving Him a drink of water. All of these actions would require a discipline in our life and when we are obedient in doing them, seems to equal fasting and that equals discipline. As fasting in our eating habits disciplines our body, so fasting in obedience to Jesus' commands disciplines our spirit. When we separate spiritual fasting and physical fasting we may begin to understand why many of the earliest text of this manuscript in Mark did not include the word fasting in its writing. This type of fasting would have to speak of spiritual fasting, as mentioned above, due to Jesus' word concerning the same event in Matthew 17:14-22. He speaks of the lack of faith as the reason the demon is not cast out and faith is only for the spiritual. Faith also is a gift that God grants and is nothing we can boast of. On the other hand, physical fasting certainly was and is many times a matter of boasting and would not give <u>God glorifying</u> spiritual power. It is also interesting how in the beginning of many of Paul's letters he mentioned in his prayers for the brothers and sisters he was addressing that he desired their love for the brethren, knowledge and understanding of God to increase more and more. As those benefits in our life become more evident along with physical and spiritual discipline, our praying and fasting will be who we are.

With this in mind might I find I am more apt to pray His will, maybe even be conformed to His image as I become more obedient and increase in faith? Then I may begin to find power in praying His will, even the power to cast out demons if and when that may be necessary. Wonder if I would even know I did it?

Almighty God, grant us the grace and mercy to discipline every aspect of our lives even as You did.

8. Praying and Fasting/Study Guide

What if God, in His infinite wisdom...

1. would tell us that when we encounter a most unusual and difficult situation that there are times when praying and fasting are necessary to resolve the event? Not to mention that He also uses that particular prescription to cast out the most difficult "demons." (Mark 9:29)

2. So what does a demon look like or sound like, and how do I even begin to know what this might mean? Well, the fasting wouldn't seem to do God any good... (Matthew 6:16-18)

3. and praying certainly allows us to speak to our Father about our concerns and needs, and it is certainly how I can let my Father know how grateful I am for ALL He has done and is doing for me, but all that is about me! But then I'm reminded of the needs of my family and friends. Oh, and God tells me to pray for workers to harvest souls... (Matthew 9:38)

4. and for other brothers and sisters to be enriched in all their speaking and in all their knowledge. (I Corinthians 1:5)

5. Might my Father know that if I discipline my eating habits (fasting) I might also find other areas of my life more disciplined? I also may realize fasting touches areas of my life other than eating, as I see what a true fast to the Father is. (Isaiah 58:6-7)

6. With this in mind, I find I am more apt to pray His will, maybe even be conformed to His image... (2 Corinthians 3:18)

7. as I become more obedient and increase in faith. Then I may begin to find power in praying His will, even the power to cast out demons if and when that may be necessary. Wonder if I would even know if I did it? (Romans 10:17)

Almighty God, grant us the grace and mercy to discipline every aspect of our lives, even as You did.

References on Praying and Fasting

1. Mark 9:29

2. Matthew 6:16-18

3. Matthew 9:38

4. 1 Corinthians 1:5

5. Isaiah 58:6-7

6. 2 Corinthians 3:18

7. Romans 10:17

Point of Truth: Praying and fasting should be the lifestyle of God's children as He directs.

Practical Application: How might I make praying and fasting the norm in my spiritual life?

CHAPTER THREE
Worship and Giving

9. Praise and Worship

What if God ordained praise from the lips of infants and children so that we might learn to praise Him and worship Him with an innocent heart without shame? We may remember that He told the woman at the well that His true worshipers would worship in spirit and truth. With that, worship must come from an obedient heart, with upright motives to exalt this "Other" being to whom we owe everything. Not only when we are singing and caught up in praise, but even in the day to day challenges that are inevitable.

Consider the activities or individuals that seem to be the most important to you. Then specify just what it is about the identified objects that interest you. Many of those things may be neutral with no harm, just a simple pastime or pleasure. However, when an activity or individual become the central focus of our lives, it may be a caution that the object has lost its definition as an interest and possibly slipping into the element of worship. When anything takes a priority to our relationship with our Creator, it has become an object of our worship. As believers, God must be the most important aspect of our lives not only at church, but all our lives, as we offer real worship. His worth must be ultimate!

That may be the real worship God seeks, every minute of every hour of every day and when we find that we wake with a song of praise on our lips and gratefulness in our heart we may be truly honoring Him with worship. Since God is a spirit might the consistent believing and trusting Him, purposing to be grateful in all things, be a work that happens in our spirit? Maybe that's when we will find ourselves anticipating the gathering of the body to worship this majestic, almighty, loving creator God and we may do so with a better understanding of spirit and truth.

You are worthy, Almighty God, to receive all praise, honor, glory and worship and may ours be a sweet smelling savor unto You.

Chapter Three
Worship and Giving

9. Praise and Worship/Study Guide

What if God...

1. ordained praise from the lips of infants and children so that we might learn to praise Him and worship Him with an innocent heart and without shame? (Psalm 8:2 & Matthew 21:16)

2. We may remember that He told the woman at the well that His true worshipers would worship Him in spirit and truth. (John 4:23-24)

3. With that, worship must come from an obedient heart, with upright motives to exalt this "Other" being to whom we owe everything. (Psalm 100 & Philippians 2:9)

4. Not only when we are singing and caught up in praise, but even in the day-to-day challenges, which are inevitable. (Proverbs 4)

5. That may be the real worship God seeks, every minute of every hour of every day, and when we find that we wake with a song of praise on our lips and gratefulness in our hearts, we may be truly honoring Him with worship. Since God is a spirit, might the consistent believing and trusting Him, purposing to be grateful in all things... (Ephesians 5:20)

6. be a work that happens in our spirit? Maybe that's when we will find ourselves anticipating the gathering of the body to worship this majestic, almighty, loving creator God, and we may do so with a better understanding of spirit and truth. (Psalm 103)

You are worthy, Almighty God, to receive all praise, honor, glory, and worship, and may ours be a sweet smelling savor unto You.

References for Praise and Worship

1. Psalm 8:2

    Matthew 21:16

2. John 4:23-24

3. Psalm 100

    Philippians 2:9

4. Proverbs 4

5. Ephesians 5:20

6. Psalm 103

Point of Truth: True worshippers of God will worship as He desires.

Practical Application: How does worshipping God in spirit and in truth become a reality in my life?

10. Adoration

What if God in receiving a wonderful exhibition of worship and love, would show us that to lavish on Him what might be labeled by the world as "very valuable", even worth a year of wages, would be but a pittance compared to what we might receive in return? Might we learn that in giving Him the things we value the most that in reality we gain more than we could ever give? Maybe what we gain is such a reverent awe of our loving, compassionate, and merciful Savior that the things we sought to gain for many years pale in comparison to the One to whom we owe everything.

Consider your most valuable possession. What is the event that might motivate you to give that possession to the Savior as an offering of your acknowledgement of who He is to you? There is no guilt here, as whatever that possession might be, your desire would be to lavish upon Him that essence without any hesitation to express your love for Jesus. As we examine our adoration of the Savior, our offering would honor Him according to His Word and we would willingly give. It is possible that valuable essence could be a most loved individual that is a part of our life and we must be willing to release that one to the Savior also as an offering.

As we look at the life of the woman that poured out this act of worship we see one who already had a heart for God. When He showed His love for her by His sorrow at the news of her brother's death, and then she realized that Jesus had purposed to allow her brother to die, that God might receive glory and also cause many to believe when Jesus miraculously raised him back to life. Later while the Savior was dining at this same family's home, this grateful woman honored Him with this all-out act of worship.

Loving Father, might we soberly peer into our own souls to see what might be restraining us from giving You our all?

10. Adoration/Study Guide

What if God, in receiving a wonderful exhibition of worship and love...

1. would show us that to lavish on Him what the world might label "very valuable," even worth a year's wages, would be but a pittance compared to what we might receive in return? (John 12:1-8)

2. Might we learn that in giving Him the things we value the most, we gain more than we could ever give? (Luke 9:25 & Matthew 16:26)

3. Maybe what we gain is such a reverent awe of our loving, compassionate, and merciful Savior that the things we sought to gain for many years pale in comparison to the One to whom we owe everything. (Ephesians 1:7-8, 2:18 & 3:12)

4. As we look at the life of the woman who poured out this act of worship, we see someone who already had a heart for God. (Luke 10:38-42)

5. When He showed His love for her by His sorrow at the news of her brother's death, and then to realize that Jesus had purposed to allow her brother to die, that God might receive glory and cause many to believe when Jesus miraculously raised him back to life. Later, while the Savior was dining at this same family's home, this grateful woman honored Him with this all-out act of worship. (John 11:1-44)

Loving Father, might we soberly peer into our own souls to see what might be restraining us from giving You our all?

References for Adoration

1. John 12:1-8

2. Luke 9:25

    Matthew 16:26

3. Ephesians 1:7-8

    Ephesians 2:18

    Ephesians 3:12

4. Luke 10:38-42

5. John 11:1-44

Point of Truth: Our worship and its potential cost reveal our true heart toward Jesus.

Practical Application: How might I be more genuine in my adoration of Jesus?

II. Giving

What if God desiring the best for His children declares the fact, the borrower is servant to the lender and reminds us that if we are giving of our blessings as He desires we will do it cheerfully? In making such requirements of His children, the all-knowing, loving Creator is fully aware that both of these truths would be the opposite of what we would naturally do. But possibly that is the nature of being His child, as He is developing in us the mind of Christ, slowly matures us to believe the principles of His word, and we realize that it is always a benefit to work and wait for the things we need, removing from our thinking the desire to impress anyone, and instead of impressing, delighting in the One to whom we owe everything.

Consider how easy it is to become enslaved to being in debt, in that a purchase as small as your smart phone can be bought on a payment plan. If your final cost is more than the selling price, you paid interest. Borrowing money for appreciating items such as houses and land, as a rule, seem to be a safe and a necessary part of living in our culture. Even an automobile, though not appreciating, is difficult to purchase without borrowing, for most. However, the principle remains and we may benefit from looking at our "want to" in comparison to our "need to". Our desire should be to honor God with our finances and realize we only own what we have completely paid for. If we haven't paid for it, we are subject to the true owner and indebted to them. So might we purpose to be freed from all debt, except our beneficent Redeemer, who is the true owner of all?

With that we may also realize that as we begin to think positively about the opportunity to support the work the church is doing, might we even get excited to be a part of helping a brother or sister in a financial difficulty to move closer to resolving their difficult matter. Especially when a note from that possibly unknown individual is received, our soul is blessed at the gratefulness of that person. How our joy may be increased to realize this is a fragrant offering, acceptable to God, and we are motivated to continue in our generosity, being cautious not to be an enabler. Might we find that being debt free makes such a thing more possible and, with such freedom, we find ourselves cheerfully giving?

Father, Your generosity was shown as You gave all for us. Enable us to walk in Your footsteps.

II. Giving/Study Guide

What if God, desiring the best for His children...

1. declares the fact that the borrower is servant to the lender... (Proverbs 22:7)

2. and reminds us that if we give of our blessings as He desires, we will do it cheerfully? (2 Corinthians 9:7)

3. In making such requirements of His children, the all-knowing, loving Creator is fully aware that both of these truths would be the opposite of what we would naturally do. (Romans 7:15)

4. That is possibly the nature of being His child, as He develops the mind of Christ in us... (Romans 12:2)

5. slowly maturing us to believe the principles of His Word, and we realize it is always a benefit to work and wait for the things we need. (Proverbs 14:23, 13:4, & Philippians 4:11)

6. Removing the desire to impress anyone from our thinking, and instead delighting in the One to whom we owe everything. (Psalm 37:4)

7. With that, we may also realize as we begin to think positively about the opportunity to support the work the church is doing, might we even get excited to be part of helping a brother or sister in a financial difficulty to move closer to resolving his or her difficult matter? (Psalm 37:21)

8. Especially when a note of gratefulness is received from the possibly unknown one we were able to bless, and our soul is blessed in increased measure at their gratitude. (Matthew 25:40)

9. How our joy may be increased to realize this is a fragrant offering, acceptable to God... (Philippians 4:14-19)

10. and we are motivated to continue our generosity, being cautious not to be an enabler. Might we find that being debt free makes such a thing more possible and that, with such freedom, we find ourselves cheerfully giving? (Romans 13:8)

Father, Your generosity was shown as You gave all for us. Enable us to walk in Your footsteps.

References for Giving

1. Proverbs 22:7

2. 2 Corinthians 9:7

3. Romans 7:15

4. Romans 12:2

5. Proverbs 14:23

   Proverbs 13:4

   Philippians 4:11

6. Psalm 37:4

7. Psalm 37:21

8. Matthew 25:40

9. Philippians 4:14-19

10. Romans 13:8

Point of Truth: Owe only the debt of love. God loves a cheerful giver.

Practical Application: How might I adjust my thinking and my lifestyle so I might give more cheerfully?

12. Possessions

What if God knowing just the amount of power money could have over all His creation would take a vulnerable widow whom evidently her resources had been consumed wrongly by the teachers of the Law? Jesus then used her as an example to all since she gave out of her need and said that her pittance given was more than all that gave out of their wealth. How sobering to think those who were entrusted as her spiritual guides had been corrupted by the love of money to the point they were blind to her needs.

Consider how quickly we can become consumed with what we want and once we get whatever it is, it can become an obsession as we want more and more, be that money or items purchased to improve what we already possess. The Jews in the account above were blinded to truth and did not realize the effect of their selfishness. Self can become an addiction just as alcohol and other substances, and when they do, recognition of such and doing something about it become lost in the obsession.

Might that cause us to look closely at all the possessions we have, realizing that those who are deceived do not see the sin they are blinded to. They don't even know they are deceived? Might we hold on loosely to possessions we have been blessed with, knowing that it is God who gives wealth and if I use that to bring Him glory, that will be evident by a generous heart, as I freely give to real needs and not worship anything other than the One True Living God.

Heavenly Father, might we grasp You with all our might as You enable us to hold on loosely to those possessions and relationships You have blessed us with, as they are all in Your hand.

12. Possessions/Study Guide

What if God, knowing just the amount of power money could have over all His creation...

1. would teach a valuable lesson using a vulnerable widow, whose resources had evidently been consumed wrongly by the teachers of the Law? (Mark 12:38-40)

2. Jesus then used her as an example to all since she gave out of her need and said her pittance given was more than all who gave out of their wealth. (Mark 12:41-44)

3. How sobering to think those who were entrusted as her spiritual guides had been corrupted by the love of money... (1 Timothy 5:3)

4. to the point they were blind to her needs. (Matthew 15:14)

5. Might that cause us to look closely at all the possessions we have, realizing that those who are blinded do not see the sin they are blinded to. They don't even know they are deceived? (Proverbs 5:6)

6. Might we hold on loosely to the possessions we have been blessed with, knowing it is God who gives wealth... (Proverbs 10:22)

7. and if I use that to bring Him glory, that will be evident by a generous heart, as I freely give to real needs and not worship anything other than the One True Living God. (1 Peter 2:12)

Heavenly Father, might we grasp you with all our might as you enable us to hold on loosely to those possessions and relationships you have blessed us with, as they are all in your hand.

References for Possessions

1. Mark 12:38-40

2. Mark 12:41-44

3. I Timothy 5:3

4. Matthew 15:14

5. Proverbs 5:6

6. Proverbs 10:22

7. I Peter 2:12

Point of Truth: The love of money is the root of all kinds of evil.

Practical Application: Do any of my possessions possess me, and do I understand I am just a steward (manager) of all I have been blessed with? Do I need to release any of my possessions?

13. Treasure

What if God in His loving wisdom reminding us that where ever our treasure is, there our heart will also be found, encourages us to store our treasures in a place that we can only read about and believe exists if we have faith? But then we may begin to realize that the treasure He speaks of is not exactly what we might normally think of as treasure. It is what our treasure should be, and since it will be stored in a different place, it may be a different kind of treasure.

Consider whatever it may be that you treasure in your life and is that person, place or thing pleasing to our Father as He also knows that it is a treasure to you? With the treasures in mind, think of them being laid at the feet of Jesus our savior and will He accept them as such?

Money certainly comes to mind when thinking of treasure, and is certainly necessary, not to mention that Solomon said, "Money is the answer for everything". Did he really mean that? Well, try to purchase anything without it, even if it is just a means of exchange. We must have something of value, even if we just swap, to gain something that is valuable to us. So is our heart captivated by money or possessions? As we ponder what our Savior really meant, it may take us to a place where our motives are initiated, the very center of our soul, where we are what we really are. Just maybe we will start to see that is the place only God and I know about and while there, might we see as He does the truly important things of the kingdom. These things may consist of the times we have shared our faith, given to that need only we were aware of, prayed for that family member that is living the life of a prodigal, or helped that widow that truly was in need. Or how about when the request came, you allowed that young girl that had decided to take her unexpected baby to full term, to live with you until the baby was delivered? Then you were there for her when she gave her precious child up to a family that had been praying for such a child knowing that she would not be able to see or hold her child for at least eighteen years, as she willingly gave him or her away. Maybe you are that girl. Now that is truly a treasure.

Loving merciful God, give us the grace to treasure You above all.

13. Treasure/Study Guide

What if God, in His loving wisdom...

1. reminding us that wherever our treasure is, there our hearts will also be found... (Matthew 6:19-21)

2. encourages us to store our treasures in a place we can only read about and believe exists if we have faith? But then we may begin to realize the treasure He speaks of is not exactly what we might normally think of as treasure. It is what our treasure should be, and since it will be stored in a different place, it may be a different kind of treasure. Money certainly comes to mind when we think of treasure, and it is certainly necessary, not to mention Solomon said, "Money is the answer for everything." (Ecclesiastes 10:19)

3. Did he really mean that? Well, try to purchase anything without it, even if it is just a means of exchange. We must have something of value, even if we just swap, to gain something that is valuable to us. So is our heart captivated by money or possessions? As we ponder what our Savior really meant, it may take us to a place where our motives are initiated, the very center of our soul, where we are what we really are. Just maybe we will start to see that is the place only God and I know about... (Matthew 9:4)

4. and while we are there, might we see as He does the truly important things of the kingdom? (Matthew 25:34-40)

5. These things may consist of the times we have shared our faith, given to that need only we were aware of, prayed for that family member who is living the life of a prodigal, or helped that widow who truly was in need. (I Timothy 5:3-8)

6. Or how about when the request came, you allowed that young girl who decided to take her unexpected baby to full term, to live with

you until the baby was delivered? Then you were there for her when she gave her precious child up to a family who had been praying for such a child knowing she would not be able to see or hold her child for at least eighteen years, as she willingly gave him or her away. Maybe you are that girl. Now that is truly a treasure. (Psalm 139:13-16)

Loving, merciful God, give us the grace to treasure You above all.

References for Treasure

1. Matthew 6:19-21

2. Ecclesiastes 10:19

3. Matthew 9:4

4. Matthew 25:34-40

5. I Timothy 5:3-8

6. Psalm 139:13-16

Point of Truth: Where your treasure is, there your heart will be also.

Practical Application: Am I storing treasures in heaven? What might they be, and how might I increase the treasury?

CHAPTER FOUR
Trials and Interaction with Others

14. Trials

What if God really loves us with a tough love and as He allows trial after trial to come into the lives of His objects of mercy knowing it is necessary to create usable vessels for His purposes? With that, our patience and perseverance may begin to increase as we become aware of our complete dependence on Him. He might also allow suffering to lead us toward obedience and humility as we finally start to realize there are reasons we are to follow the principles and commands found in His word.

Consider that difficulties and problems are the last thing any of us want to go through and our tendency is to avoid such if there is any way possible to escape a trial. However, God knowing that suffering is the vehicle that teaches His children to walk in obedience, steadily allows trials and test to enter our lives. Each trial is specifically designed to drag us a little closer to His likeness. As we grow a little older and mature in the faith we can look back and see how the Father has patiently done this work. Possibly we began as a person with an impatient temperament that tends to be very self reliant and proud and through specific trials He transforms them into a person that understands he or she is dependent on God for everything and in every circumstance. What began as an impatient, volatile personality is supernaturally transformed into a personality with a patient; balanced spirit that understands life is all about walking and living in Jesus. And even with this amazing change, the loving Father still sends life changing trials and tests to make us even closer to His likeness. Seems the key to the change has a lot to do with our response, resisting or embracing the trial. Trials and test are coming if we are truly His children and He will accomplish His work in us.

Maybe if we would truly allow Him to have even the parts of us we have been clinging to for years, we would discover that they are the idols that He so detests, because we value them more than Him, and that is why we have been clinging to them. So maybe when we reach this point and humble ourselves, we may find He will pour more and more grace into our lives. Might this cause us to increase our desire to fellowship (prayer) with Him, which in turn brings about a desire to truly and humbly worship this holy, loving God?

Father, may we trust You, that You are truly good, and as You allow trials and tests, give us the grace to embrace them and not resist or resent them.

Chapter Four
Trials and Interaction with Others

14. Trials/Study Guide

What if God really loves us with a tough love...

1. and He allows trial after trial to come into the lives of His objects of mercy knowing they are necessary to create usable vessels for His purposes? (Romans 9:23)

2. With that, our patience and perseverance may begin to increase as we become aware of our complete dependence on Him. (James 1:2-4)

3. He might also allow suffering... (1 Peter 4:12-13)

4. to lead us toward obedience... (Hebrews 5:8)

5. and humility... (Proverbs 3:34)

6. as we finally start to realize there are reasons we are to follow the principles and commands in His Word. (Proverbs 7:2)

7. Maybe if we would truly allow Him to have even the parts of us we have been clinging to for years, we would discover they are the idols He so detests because we value them more than we value Him, and that is why we have been clinging to them. (Colossians 3:5-6)

8. So maybe when we reach this point and humble ourselves, we may find He will pour more and more grace into our lives. Might this cause us to increase our desire to fellowship (pray) with Him, which in turn brings about a desire to truly and humbly worship this holy, loving God? (James 4:6 & 1 Peter 5:5-7)

Father, may we trust You, that You are truly good, and as You allow trials and tests, give us the grace to embrace them and not resist or resent them.

References for Trials

1. Romans 9:23

2. James 1:2-4

3. I Peter 4:12-13

4. Hebrews 5:8

5. Proverbs 3:34

6. Proverbs 7:2

7. Colossians 3:5-6

8. James 4:6

   I Peter 5:5-7

Point of Truth: God, in love, will allow trials and tests in our lives to mold us, as God's vessels, into usable vessels.

Practical Application: How might I embrace present and coming trials and tests instead of resisting them?

15. Voice of the Shepherd / Witnessing

What if God tells us to go into our world and speak His word knowing that His sheep will recognize the voice of their shepherd and they will at some point be gathered into the fold ... all His sheep? He is the enabler and Savior; we simply speak the message. Regardless of resistance Sovereignty will overcome resistance?

Consider in Protestant circles, there are two views taught as to how these sheep are brought into the fold. One says that we are spiritually dead in our trespasses and sins, but still can hear, with ears of flesh, the voice of the shepherd when He calls. Then, still spiritually dead, we, with our free will choose to believe Jesus is who He says He is. And because of our choice we are born again, made alive spiritually and become a sheep in the shepherd's fold. The other view taught is that we are, as the other view, spiritually dead in our trespasses and sins from birth. However, God, in His Sovereignty, has predestined and chosen His sheep from before the creation of the world according to His will and pleasure. Then as the Spirit wills, that same Holy Spirit, regenerates (makes alive) His sheep. Once we are born again (made alive) spiritually, we now can hear the Spirit's effectual call and we believe as God had ordained. These views have been simplified, but they have divided believers for centuries and as you seek God, and the Word says no one seeks God in the flesh but all in the flesh are God-haters, may you determine how one is brought into the Shepherd's fold. Neither view changes the Lord's command to make disciples. The Samaritan woman at the well and the demoniac of the Garasenes are good examples of sheep being brought into the fold by the Good Shepherd, and their responses should also be ours.

Now, that should free us to do as the Samaritan woman or the man of the Garasenes that was freed from demon possession. She went back to her village and simply told what Jesus had done in her life and many believed in the Savior because of her testimony. After the earlier-mentioned demoniac was redeemed, he asked if he could go with Jesus (on a mission trip) and was instructed to simply go home and tell what Jesus had done for him. Might that also mean we have the opportunity where ever we are to be willing to share what Messiah has done for us, whether we are in our Jerusalem, Judea, Samaria or the ends of the earth? If you are called to do more you will be miserable until you answer the call, so trust Him, and be willing to do whatever He asks. Salvation is of the Lord and what a privilege to be a tool in that work!

Lord, give us grace to be bold as we are obedient to Your command to make disciples.

15. Voice of the Shepherd (Witnessing)/Study Guide

What if God tells us to go into our world and speak His Word...

1. knowing His sheep will recognize the voice of their shepherd and they will, at some point, be gathered into the fold? (John 10:1-18)

2. All His sheep? (John 6:37)

3. He is the enabler... (John 6:65)

4. and the Savior; we simply speak the message. Regardless of resistance, Sovereignty will overcome resistance. (Romans 9:19)

5. Now, that should free us to do as the Samaritan woman... (John 4:39)

6. or the man of Garasenes, who was freed from demon possession. She went back to her village and simply told what Jesus had done in her life, and many believed in the Savior because of her testimony. (John 4:39-42)

7. After the earlier-mentioned demoniac was redeemed, he asked if he could go with Jesus (on a mission trip) and was instructed to simply go home and tell what Jesus had done for him. (Mark 5:18-20)

8. Might that also mean we have the opportunity wherever we are to be willing to share what the Messiah has done for us, whether we are in our Jerusalem, Judea, Samaria, or the ends of the earth? (Acts 1:8)

9. If you are called to do more, you will be miserable until you answer the call, so trust Him, and be willing to do whatever He asks. (Philippians 4:8-9)

10. Salvation is of the Lord, and what a privilege to be a tool in that work! (Psalm 37:39)

Lord, give us grace to be bold as we are obedient to Your command to make disciples.

References for Voice of the Shepherd/Witnessing

1. John 10:1-18
2. John 6:37
3. John 6:65
4. Romans 9:19
5. John 4:39
6. John 4:39-42
7. Mark 5:18-20
8. Acts 1:8
9. Philippians 4:8-9
10. Psalm 37:39

Point of Truth: Sheep will recognize their Shepherd's voice.

Practical Application: How might I be more motivated to share what Jesus has done for me, considering these truths?

16. Relationships

What if God loves us so much, He tells us we must "hate" all those here, that we love the most just to be worthy of Him? Not fully understanding, but wanting to be obedient, we find when we truly embrace such a difficult task we begin to understand that loving Him like He says makes us so tender at heart that we may begin to love all those we meet, not just those we should love. With that, our mind begins to become more like His mind and our eyes see as His eyes.

Consider those in your life you love the most and measure that love if possible. That measurement should seem small compared to how we are instructed to love our Savior. When realizing Jesus said if we fall short of this love for Him, we are not worthy of Him, it becomes sobering indeed. To have this love for Jesus, one must realize the importance of Him choosing us to be His child and from that realization, truly trust Him to be who and what He says He is. He is holy, perfect, and just in everything He does. That means everything that happens to believers has a purpose and is good and that may mean letting go of those we love the most to a degree if that love interferes with our relationship to Jesus. Each individual will have to apply this principle personally and seek God in understanding it more clearly.

The sin He so hates because of the destruction that always is not far behind becomes much less alluring, even disgusting, and it breaks our heart in those we love the most. We may even find ourselves realizing we may be required to spend eternity without some of those we love the most if they never turn from wickedness, even though we may pray diligently for their salvation, and know for a fact that we ourselves may have shared the good news of Jesus Christ with those loved ones. So maybe that's something to do with a peace that passes all understanding. At this point we may truly begin to obey His commands, for they are not a burden.

Lord Jesus, may we love You above all and enable us to show mercy as we look through Your eyes of eternity.

16. Relationships/Study Guide

What if God loves us so much...

1. that He tells us we must "hate" all those we love the most, just to be worthy of Him? (Luke 14:26 & Matthew 10:37)

2. Not fully understanding, but wanting to be obedient, we find when we truly embrace such a difficult task, we begin to understand that loving Him like He says makes us so tender at heart that we may begin to love all those we meet... (I Thessalonians 3:12)

3. not just those we should love. With that, our minds begin to become more like His mind, and our eyes see as His eyes. (I Corinthians 2:16)

4. The sin He so hates because of the destruction that is always not far behind becomes much less alluring, even disgusting, and it breaks our hearts in those we love the most. (Proverbs 8:7 & 13)

5. We may even find ourselves realizing we may be required to spend eternity without some of those we love the most if they never turn from wickedness, even though we may pray diligently for their salvation, and know for a fact that we ourselves may have shared the good news of Jesus Christ with those loved ones. So maybe that has something to do with a peace that passes all understanding. (Philippians 4:6-7)

6. At this point, we may truly begin to obey His commands, for they are not a burden. (I John 5:3)

Lord Jesus, may we love You above all. Enable us to show mercy as we look through Your eyes of eternity.

References for Relationships

1. Luke 14:26

    Matthew 10:37

2. I Thessalonians 3:12

3. I Corinthians 2:16

4. Proverbs 8:7 & 13

5. Philippians 4:6-7

6. I John 5:3

Point of Truth: We must love God supremely, above all.

Practical Application: Is there anything in my life I may love more than Jesus Christ, and, if so, how might I love that less and Jesus more?

17. Forgiveness

What if God, knowing just how difficult it would be for His creation to truly overlook the offenses we would enact upon each other, would provide grace to be obedient when we humble ourselves and obey? Unwillingness to forgive is the trait that would lead to seemingly unending hurt and pain, scheming and wars. Even in His Law it seems that retribution is His will, as an eye for an eye and a tooth for a tooth is part of that Law. But just maybe His Law, revealing He is just, merciful, orderly, compassionate, and loving, while also full of wrath for the wicked, states that He will repay evil with vengeance. Wow, and Jesus commands His followers to love those who treat us wrongly and to show compassion to the wicked, even giving and providing sustenance to them.

Consider how opposite of our natural tendencies true forgiveness is. It is something that can only happen as God softens our new heart and we realize the scope of His forgiveness to us. The realization that no one would be redeemed without the mercy and pity God has shown us in enabling us to see our lost condition and then granting repentance out of His mercy. Being mindful of such mercy we have no allowance for not granting the same mercy.

Did God change from the Old Testament to the New Testament? Or maybe in revealing Himself before He came to purchase His chosen people, He was showing that He really is just and He would repay evil, freeing us from such a chore, and thus giving us an incentive to forgive and to be able to receive His forgiveness. Maybe this is a sign that we really are His children and this truth of giving forgiveness as a condition for receiving forgiveness would allow us to grow in compassion for the lost. And just maybe when we are tempted to judge their wickedness, might we remember they are only doing the will of their master and if we show them love, they might be part of us who have turned and received forgiveness.

Merciful forgiving Father, empower us to understand the importance and necessity of being forgiving in all things.

17. Forgiveness/Study Guide

What if God, knowing just how difficult it would be for His creation to truly overlook the offenses we enact upon each other...

1. would provide grace to be obedient when we humble ourselves and obey? Unwillingness to forgive... (Matthew 6:15)

2. is the trait that leads to seemingly unending hurt and pain, scheming, and wars. Even in His Law it seems that retribution is His will, as an eye for an eye and a tooth for a tooth is part of that Law. (Deuteronomy 19:21)

3. But just maybe His Law, revealing He is just, merciful, orderly, compassionate, and loving, while also full of wrath for the wicked... (Romans 1:18-20)

4. states that He will repay evil with vengeance. Wow, and Jesus commands His followers to love those who treat us wrongly and to show compassion to the wicked, even giving and providing sustenance to them. (Matthew 5:39-42)

5. Did God change from the Old Testament to the New Testament? Or maybe in revealing Himself before He came to purchase His chosen people, He was showing He really is just and He would repay evil... (Romans 12:19-20)

6. freeing us from such a chore, and thus giving us an incentive to forgive and to be able to receive His forgiveness. (Luke 6:37)

7. Maybe this is a sign that we really are His children and giving forgiveness as a condition for receiving forgiveness would allow us to grow in compassion for the lost. And just maybe when we are tempted to judge their wickedness... (Romans 2:1)

8. might we remember they are only doing the will of their master? If we show them love, they might be part of us who have turned and received forgiveness. (John 8:44 & 2 Timothy 2:26)

Merciful forgiving Father, empower us to understand the importance and necessity of being forgiving in all things.

References for Forgiveness

1. Matthew 6:15

2. Deuteronomy 19:21

3. Romans 1:18-20

4. Matthew 5:39-42

5. Romans 12:19-20

6. Luke 6:37

7. Romans 2:1

8. John 8:44

    2 Timothy 2:26

Point of Truth: We must forgive others who have wronged us to receive God's forgiveness.

Practical Application: Is there someone in my life to whom I owe the debt of forgiveness?

18. Anxieties

What if God lovingly reminds us that a peace that passes human understanding awaits us even when we would tend to be anxious concerning the more difficult matters we face in life? He even led Paul, the one writing His truth, to speak of his own anxieties. As we ponder these things, that is a bit of a relief knowing Paul encouraged us not to be anxious but had to be stretched to actually walk in this place. Maybe to be able to walk there, we would need to focus on the One who holds every event in His hand and then we may be reminded that we are to be communicating with this One always. Now in that communication might we start seeking to know Him better and realize the only place I find His personality is in His word. So might we study Him more, talk to Him more and even speak His word back to Him as we think more like Him.

Consider the natural anxiety that a parent would have the first time their son or daughter leave the house and drive to a destination. We quickly realize, we are suddenly helpless and our control of the situation is no more. We are blessed to have the opportunity to pray and call on the Controller of all things for protection of that maturing child. But the fact is the older they get the control factor we have becomes less and less. That seems a very good time to realize our complete dependence on Him. Then if that call or message comes with difficult or even unbelievable news concerning that loved one, hopefully we have matured to the point that we know God is in and above all, and as we lean strongly into Him, He is there and His comfort is available as we trust and depend on Him.

It does seem the things we care about the most, like our children, grown or not; and other loved ones, and the events concerning them are the situations that cause us to be anxious the most. So might there need to be a conscious and intentional effort to give thanksgiving and offer prayers in faith concerning those difficult situations and purpose to trust God that He is working all things for our good? But in doing so might we find that a peace that is beyond our understanding will be more the norm than being anxious?

God, You are our Strong Tower so may we give all our anxious thoughts to You.

18. Anxieties/Study Guide

What if God lovingly reminds us...

1. that a peace that passes human understanding awaits us even when we would tend to be anxious concerning the more difficult matters we face in life? (Philippians 4:6-7)

2. He even led Paul, the one writing His truth, to speak of his own anxieties. (Philippians 2:28, 1984 NIV)

3. As we ponder these things, it is a bit of a relief to know that Paul encouraged us not to be anxious and had to be stretched to actually walk in that place. Maybe to be able to walk there, we would need to focus on the One who holds every event in His hand... (I Timothy 6:13-15)

4. and then we may be reminded that we are to be communicating with this One always. (I Thessalonians 5:16-18)

5. Now, in that communication, might we start seeking to know Him better... (Proverbs 8:17)

6. and realize the only place I find His personality is in His Word. So might we study Him more, talk to Him more, and even speak His Word back to Him as we think more like Him? It does seem the things we care about the most, like our children, grown or not; other loved ones; and the events concerning them are the situations that cause us to be anxious the most. So might there need to be a conscious and intentional effort to give thanksgiving and offer prayers in faith... (James 5:15)

7. concerning those difficult situations and purpose to trust God that He is working all things for our good? (Romans 8:28)

8. But in doing so, might we find that a peace that is beyond our understanding... (John 14:27)

will be more the norm than being anxious?

God, You are our Strong Tower so may we give all our anxious thoughts to You.

References for Anxieties

1. Philippians 4:6-7

2. Philippians 2:28, 1984 (NIV)

3. I Timothy 6:13-15

4. I Thessalonians 5:16-18

5. Proverbs 8:17

6. James 5:15

7. Romans 8:28

8. John 14:27

Point of Truth: Worries and anxieties mean taking on responsibilities God doesn't intend for us to deal with.

Practical Application: What causes me to be anxious and how might I cast all my cares and worries on Jesus?

CHAPTER FIVE

Discernment

19. Making Wise Judgments

What if God in His omniscience sternly reminds us through His half-brother's pen that we would always have to deal with the temptation to judge each other in the body? But also we might remember that Paul told us that it is our duty to judge those in the body? And what about Jesus saying do not judge, or you will be judged, measured to you the same measure you used to judge? Jesus also said to remove the log in your own eye; then you can see clearly to remove the speck in your brother's eye! But since Jesus also told us we would have to make judgments, might He be giving us the correct measuring tool to use when we have to make those judgments, namely His Word? That is what believers will be measured by.

Consider how we are often tempted to think wrongly of a brother or sister when we see something that strikes as wrong. This is the work of our enemy desiring to be divisive in the body and it works. In the spirit of love and unity, we must make every effort to resist these wrong temptations and think correctly in our judgments.

Might James, Paul and Jesus be speaking of the types of things the world gets caught up in judging, concerning each other, like what someone eats, how educated someone is, how rich or poor someone is, how someone wears his or her hair, the price of clothes someone wears, the type automobile a person may drive, the type home he or she may live in or whether a person owes money or how much. This list might go on and on, and these things may certainly affect our lifestyles, which will be effected by how we apply God's principles to things such as modest dress and the command not to owe anyone, save the debt of love which we owe everyone.

It does seem that the pivot point on judging in the body has to do with known sin and that sin being addressed by those to whom the responsibility is assigned, namely those who are spiritually mature in a family and/or those in authority in the church. The temptation to judge the things as the world does, things that are usually petty at best and tend to cause fights and quarrels should not even come into play in the body that is commanded to love each other with the love of Christ. We are even commanded that we <u>must</u> love, and at times that love may mean addressing known sin! As our loving Abba Father reminds us of these things, might we realize how important it is to act carefully and lovingly in all situations as we, by His grace, are conformed to His image.

Father, You are the Judge of all souls, and may we walk cautiously as we may be called on to exercise judgment.

Chapter Five
Discernment

19. Making Wise Judgments/Study Guide

What if God, in His omniscience...

1. sternly reminds us through His half-brother's pen that we would always have to deal with the temptation to judge each other in the body? (James 2:4 & 4:11-12)

2. But might we also remember that Paul told us it is our duty to judge those in the body? (I Corinthians 5:12-13)

3. And what about Jesus saying, do not judge, or you will be judged, measured to you the same measure you used to judge? Jesus also said to remove the log in your own eye; then you can see clearly to remove the speck in your brother's eye! (Matthew 7:1-5)

4. But since Jesus also told us we would have to make judgments, might He be giving us the correct measuring tool to use when we have to make those judgments, namely His Word? That is what believers will be measured by. Might James, Paul, and Jesus be speaking of the types of things the world gets caught up in judging, concerning each other, like what someone eats, how educated someone is, how rich or poor someone is, how someone wears his or her hair, the price of clothes someone wears, the type automobile a person may drive, the type of home he or she may live in, or whether a person owes money and how much. This list might go on and on, and these things... (James 4:1-6 & Romans 14:10-13)

5. may certainly affect our lifestyles, which will be effected by how we apply God's principles to things such as modest dress... (I Timothy 2:9-10)

6. and the command not to owe anyone, save the debt of love we owe everyone. (Romans 13:8)

7. It does seem that the pivot point on judging in the body has to do with known sin… (I Corinthians 5:6-11)

8. and that sin being addressed by those to whom the responsibility is assigned, namely those who are spiritually mature in a family and those in authority in the church. (Galatians 6:1-5)

9. The temptation to judge the things as the world does, things that are usually petty at best and tend to cause fights and quarrels, should not even come into play in the body… (James 4:1-11)

10. that is commanded to love each other with the love of Christ. (I John 4:7-12)

11. We are even commanded that we <u>must</u> love, and at times that love may mean addressing known sin! As our loving Abba Father reminds us of these things, might we realize how important it is to act carefully and lovingly in all situations, as we, by His grace, are conformed to His image. (I John 4:21 & John 13:34)

Father, You are the Judge of all souls, and may we walk cautiously in case we are called on to exercise judgment.

References for Making Wise Judgments

1. James 2:4

    James 4:11-12

2. I Corinthians 5:12-13

3. Matthew 7:1-5

4. James 4:1-6

    Romans 14:10-13

5. I Timothy 2:9-10

6. Romans 13:8

7. I Corinthians 5:6-11

8. Galatians 6:1-5

9. James 4:1-11

10. I John 4:7-12

11. I John 4:21

    John 13:34

Point of Truth: Judging each other as the world does only harms the body and brings judgment on ourselves.

Practical Application: How have I been tempted to judge brothers and sisters concerning unimportant matters as mentioned?

20. Truth, Love, and Judgment

What if God knowing the tension that would always come when the truth of the Word and love that is commanded in the Word come into seeming conflict in the same situation? Maybe He knew when we come to full knowledge of a sinful situation; we tend to overlook certain glaring problems that may need to be dealt with. We are told not to judge the <u>world</u> while we are here as aliens because that's His job, but we are reminded that it is the difficult task of authority, whether it be in the church or in families, to make wise judgments concerning those who are part of the church when His Word is violated.

Considering the seriousness of the subject, let's carefully unwrap what is here. We may often find ourselves confronted with sinful situations as we go about our daily lives, but as a rule these involve unbelievers and we are instructed not to judge their sin. This may be something as deviant as homosexuality, but, we are commanded not to judge the unbeliever in their sin. God will do that! We are instructed to love them and if the opportunity arises to tell them what Jesus has done in our lives. We are also to do the same with those unbelievers that appear good. Our merciful Father says their goodness and our goodness, in His view, are filthy disease-ridden rags. Only because we have been born again and are imputed with Jesus Christ's righteousness, are we considered righteous! This is a work of God alone and completely undeserved. Why us? That is the unanswerable question, but how it should cause us to stand in awe of the Sovereign God and His mercy. Now we will address the sin question, only among believers, only known sin that is harmful to another believer, or the body as a whole. This may, for example be an individual in the church that is involved in infidelity and it has been made known and he or she is unrepentant. It must be addressed, by church leadership as is prescribed in next week's devotion. It may also be one's adult son or daughter that claim Christ and are living in unrepentant sin of which their parent is aware. It must be addressed also, but here it would be best by family authority, Father or Father and Mother and possibly it will have to go no further if the individual responds and God grants repentance.

Wow, ok, it's not a contradiction; we are not to judge, but we must judge! Then He reminds us that <u>we will</u> judge the world at some point in His kingdom, and not only that, but we will judge angels too! Think I got it; we need the mind of Christ and You to grant us grace though humility to soberly walk in obedience and to be full of grace and mercy in doing so.

Merciful Father, grant us grace, through humility, to soberly walk in obedience and to be full of grace and mercy as You are.

20. Truth, Love, and Judgment/Study Guide

What if God...

1. has always known the tension that would always come when the truth of the Word and the love commanded in the Word seem to come into conflict in the same situation? Maybe He knew when we come into full knowledge of a sinful situation, we tend to overlook certain glaring problems that may need to be dealt with. We are told not to judge the <u>world</u> while we are here as aliens because... (Romans 2:3 & Matthew 7:1-2)

2. that's His job, but we are reminded that the difficult task of authority, whether it be in the church or in families, is to make wise judgments concerning those who are part of the church when His Word is violated. Wow, ok, it's not a contradiction; we are not to judge, but we must judge! (I Corinthians 5:1-13)

3. Then He reminds us <u>we will</u> judge the world at some point in His kingdom, and not only that, but we will judge angels, too! (I Corinthians 6:1-3)

4. Think I got it; we need the mind of Christ... (I Corinthians 2:16)

5. and You to grant us grace through humility to soberly walk in obedience and to be full of grace and mercy in doing so. (Hosea 6:6 & James 3:17)

Merciful Father, grant us the grace, through humility, to soberly walk in obedience and to be full of grace and mercy as You are.

References for Truth, Love, and Judgment

1. Romans 2:3

    Matthew 7:1-2

2. I Corinthians 5:1-13

3. I Corinthians 6:1-3

4. I Corinthians 2:16

5. Hosea 6:6

    James 3:17

Point of Truth: As believers, we must judge correctly, as it affects the whole body of Christ.

Practical Application: Might I tend to overlook sin that causes me to compromise the Word? Note: This only applies to believers.

21. Truth, Love, and Compassion

What if God knowing we would need His mind in situations involving the tension between truth and love; the starting place might be to look deep within ourselves at our own sinfulness, to be sure our motives are pure and we are clean before our Maker? A situation like this is hopefully rarely encountered, and possibly for some will never be. If it is encountered, however, and needs addressing, fortunately we have been given a prescription to follow.

It is always best if this can be handled one on one and resolved by admonishing our brother with a careful warning. This will allow minimum recognition by the body and hopefully avoid unnecessary shame and embarrassment. But if the individual continues to be unrepentant, the Lord did not say, "Don't worry about it; everything will be alright." What He did say was to continue to pursue the situation, and, if needed, to carefully choose another brother or sister, and humbly, kindly, gently, carefully and in love, address the area of sin and pray that God would provide the means for repentance. Making every effort to forgive and observe true repentance in that brother or sister that is caught up in known sin.

Consider, we are commanded to first go to the brother or sister one on one, then if necessary to take one or two other witnesses along. Then after this effort to keep the matter low key and as discreet as possible the Lord said to make the matter public before the whole church.

Does God really say that if that brother or sister refuses to repent that we are to treat them as if they are not really a brother or sister? You mean that brother or sister would repent if he or she were truly regenerated? After the means to restore this brother or sister are exhausted we should still pray and always be open to repentance and for the body to restore him or her, even though that person's actions seem to point to the possibility he or she is not a brother or sister at all. That being the case, how do we go about such a difficult task? God will empower when this is necessary and if He is willing there will be repentance, but might we use extreme care and caution if we find ourselves involved in such a situation. It does seem that if we are to truly honor our holy God, we will realize just how evil and repulsive sin in His body is, and when it stares us in the face because we see clearly, it cannot be overlooked. We must act with His grace to see with His eyes and to love as He loves to truly show justice, mercy, faithfulness and humility!

Father these are difficult truths, how we need You to enable us to accept them and empower us to be bold and courageous in walking out Your truth.

21. Truth, Love, and Compassion/Study Guide

What if God, knowing that we would need His mind in situations involving the tension between truth and love...

1. the starting place might be to look deep within ourselves at our own sinfulness... (Matthew 7:3-5)

2. to be sure our motives are pure and we are clean before our Maker? (Psalm 51:1-4 & 66:18)

3. A situation like this is hopefully rarely encountered, and possibly for some will never be. If it is encountered, however, and needs addressing, fortunately God has given us a prescription to follow. (Matthew 18:15-18)

4. It is always best to resolve the situation one on one by admonishing our brother with a careful warning. This will allow minimum recognition by the body and hopefully avoid unnecessary shame and embarrassment. But if the individual continues to be unrepentant, the Lord did not say, "Don't worry about it; everything will be all right." What He did say was to continue to pursue the situation, and, if needed, to carefully choose another brother or sister, and humbly, kindly, gently, carefully, and in love, address the area of sin... (Galatians 6:1)

5. and pray that God would provide the means for repentance. (Acts 11:18)

6. Making every effort to forgive and observe true repentance in that brother or sister who is caught up in known sin. Does God really say if that brother or sister refuses to repent that we are to treat him or her as if he or she is not really a brother or sister? (Matthew 18:17)

7. You mean that brother or sister would repent if he or she were truly regenerated? (1 John 3:6)

8. After the means to restore this brother or sister are exhausted, we should still pray and always be open for that person to repent and for the body to restore him or her, even though that person's actions seem to point to the possibility he or she is not a brother or sister at all. That being the case, how do we go about such a difficult task? God will empower when this is necessary... (Philippians 4:19)

9. and if He is willing, there will be repentance... (2 Corinthians 2:5-10 & 2 Timothy 2:25)

10. but might we use extreme care and caution if we find ourselves involved in such a situation? It does seem that if we are to truly honor our holy God, we will realize just how evil and repulsive sin in His body is, and when it stares us in the face because we see clearly, we cannot overlook it. (1 Corinthians 5:6-7)

11. We must act with His grace to see with His eyes... (2 Corinthians 8:21)

12. and to love as He loves to truly show justice, mercy, faithfulness, and humility! (James 4:6 & Matthew 23:23)

Father, these are difficult truths. How we need You to enable us to accept them and empower us to be bold and courageous in walking out Your truth.

References for Truth, Love, and Compassion

1. Matthew 7:3-5

2. Psalm 51:1-4

   Psalm 66:18

3. Matthew 18:15-18

4. Galatians 6:1

5. Acts 11:18

6. Matthew 18:17

7. 1 John 3:6

8. Philippians 4:19

9. 2 Corinthians 2:5-10

   2 Timothy 2:25

10. 1 Corinthians 5:6-7

11. 2 Corinthians 8:21

12. James 4:6

    Matthew 23:23

Point of Truth: Mature believers must make every effort to judge correctly, especially concerning matters that violate the Word of God, and act accordingly.

Practical Application: Am I clean (log free) before my Maker, and am I adding to the purity of the body?

CHAPTER SIX
OLD COVENANT APPLICATION TO CONTEMPORARY LIFE

22. Diet

What if God wanting His children to be healthy physically, mentally and spiritually reveals to us that one of the keys to that healthiness, in His Law, was telling the Hebrews not to eat certain types of meat? The Almighty Creator God, knowing the purpose for each of the animals He created, called some clean and some unclean. But then the Messiah revealed that it is not what goes into the body that makes it clean or unclean, but the heart is revealed by what is spoken. He probably wasn't talking about the physical body, was He? So did God's creation change with the covenant of Messiah and the atonement for sin? Also, Peter's vision seemed to point out that we could eat anything freely. Is it possible that he was speaking more about the Gentiles being welcomed into the new covenant of Jesus? Maybe God, knowing what an issue food might become, says certainly the Law is now fulfilled and what you eat is completely up to you.

Consider that in some circles what you eat is a measure of how holy you are. This is in no way what the Lord would have intended, as it is divisive. But there are studies that lend evidence to the fact that the Creator's diet is beneficial and some of what is mentioned below gives a hint as to why.

As we reflect on His Law, might it just be possible that freely using the Creator's diet as a guide to a healthy body, soul and mind might still have certain benefits, as we realize most of the unclean animals/fish themselves would eat a different diet than the clean animals and process their food differently? He designed some of the animals/fish as simply garbage disposals, while He designed others to clean up what was killed and left. Those called "clean" seemed to prefer grass and chewed cud, had a completely divided hoof. The clean fish, however, had fins and scales and tended to feed on other fish instead of cleaning up the bottom of the ocean as some fish and other water creatures do. Is it possible those differences could cause certain animals to be healthier for humans to consume? Once again, as we, His children, study His word, and as we mature, might find it profitable to discipline another area of our lives, and in doing so, benefit once again by the Creator's design.

Creator God, let us see all of Your Word as a benefit to our lives.

Chapter Six
Old Covenant Application to Contemporary Life

22. Diet/Study Guide

What if God...

1. wanting His children to be physically, mentally, and spiritually healthy... (3 John 1:2-4)

2. reveals to us that one of the keys to that healthiness, in His Law, was telling the Hebrews not to eat certain types of meat? The Almighty Creator God, knowing the purpose for each animal He created, called some clean and some unclean. (Leviticus 11:1-24)

3. But then the Messiah revealed it is not what goes into the body that makes it clean or unclean, but the heart is revealed by what is spoken. He probably wasn't talking about the physical body, was He? (Matthew 15:11)

4. So did God's creation change with the covenant of the Messiah and the atonement for sin? Also, Peter's vision seemed to point out that we could eat anything freely. Is it possible that he was speaking more about the Gentiles being welcomed into the new covenant of Jesus? (Acts 11:1-21)

5. Maybe God, knowing what an issue food might become... (Romans 14:1-4)

6. says certainly the Law is now fulfilled... (Matthew 5:17)

7. and what you eat is completely up to you. As we reflect on His Law, might it just be possible that freely using the Creator's diet as a guide to a healthy body, soul, and mind might still have certain benefits, as we realize most of the unclean animals/fish themselves

would eat a different diet than the clean animals and process their food differently? He designed some of the animals/fish as simply garbage disposals, while He designed others to clean up what was killed and left. Those called "clean" seemed to prefer grass, chewed cud, and had a completely divided hoof. The clean fish, however, had fins and scales and tended to feed on other fish instead of cleaning up the bottom of the ocean as some fish and other water creatures do. Is it possible those differences could cause certain animals to be healthier for humans to consume? Once again, as we, His children, study His Word, and as we mature, might we find it profitable to discipline another area of our lives, and in doing so, benefit once again by the Creator's design? (Psalm 19:7)

Creator God, let us see all of Your Word as a benefit to our lives.

References for Diet

1. 3 John 1:2-4

2. Leviticus 11:1-24

3. Matthew 15:11

4. Acts 11:1-21

5. Romans 14:1-4

6. Matthew 5:17

7. Psalm 19:7

Point of Truth: God's Word does not change. It is eternal, as He is.

Practical Application: In what ways might I improve my diet?

23. God's Power

What if God desiring to make known His power to the people of the world, would impress upon His prophet to challenge the prophets of Baal to a contest to prove which god is truly God? The Almighty Omnipotent, Omniscient One was in the midst of judging His people, the majority of whom had abandoned His laws and commands, with a drought that had gone on for three-plus years, so water was scarce at best. The challenge God's prophet and Baal's prophets had was to offer a bull for a sacrifice. The god that consumed the bull with fire was truly God.

Consider the difference this one man made empowered by the Almighty God and the position he put himself in by making such a challenge. He knew God, but more importantly God knew him, and used him to accomplish His purposes.

Going first the prophets of Baal cried out, danced, shouted and cut themselves, as was their custom, until their blood flowed. God's prophet taunted them to shout louder to wake their god. Then the prophet rose and commanded his bull, the altar and the ditch that had been dug to hold the water, be drenched three times with jars of water, perhaps sea water since fresh was scarce. Next, he prayed a simple two-sentence prayer to the true God: "O Lord, God of Abraham, Isaac and Israel, let it be known today that You are God in Israel and that I am Your servant and have done all these things at Your command. Answer me, O Lord, answer me, so these people will know that You, O Lord, are God, and that You are turning their hearts back again." (I Kings 18:36-37) Fire fell from heaven and consumed the sacrifice, the wood, the stones, and the soil and licked up the water. Now that is powerful! Might it be important that by spending time in our prayer closet privately with the One to whom we are praying, we will be better prepared when we pray, especially in public. In doing so, might we be more likely to pray His will, so that prayer will more likely be effective? My truck seems to make a pretty good prayer closet since I spend a lot of time in it. But might we find the more we pray, the more we want to converse with this all-powerful Being, no matter where we find ourselves?

Omnipotent God, may we honor You with our words, to others and to You.

23. God's Power/Study Guide

What if God, desiring to make known His power to the people of the world...

1. would impress upon His prophet to challenge the prophets of Baal to a contest to prove which god is truly God? The Almighty Omnipotent, Omniscient One was in the midst of judging His people, the majority of whom had abandoned His laws and commands, with a drought that had gone on for three-plus years, so water was scarce at best. The challenge God's prophet and Baal's prophets had was to offer a bull for a sacrifice. The god that consumed the bull with fire was truly God.

   Going first, the prophets of Baal cried out, danced, shouted, and cut themselves, as was their custom, until their blood flowed. God's prophet taunted them to shout louder to wake their god. Then the prophet rose and commanded his bull, the altar, and the ditch that had been dug to hold the water be drenched three times with large jars of water, perhaps sea water since fresh was scarce.

   Next, he prayed a simple two-sentence prayer to the true God: "O Lord, God of Abraham, Isaac and Israel, let it be known today that You are God in Israel and that I am Your servant and have done all these things at Your command. Answer me, O Lord, answer me, so these people will know that You, O Lord, are God, and that You are turning their hearts back again." Fire fell from heaven and consumed the sacrifice, the wood, the stones, and the soil, and licked up the water. (I Kings 18:16-45)

2. Now that is powerful! Might it be important that by spending time in our prayer closet privately with the One to whom we are praying, so that we will be better prepared when we pray, especially in public... (Matthew 6:5-15)

3. and in doing so, might we be more likely to pray His will, so that prayer will more likely be effective? My truck seems to make a pretty good prayer closet since I spend a lot of time in it. But might we find the more we pray, the more we want to converse with this all-powerful Being, no matter where we find ourselves? (James 5:13-18)

Omnipotent God, may we honor You with our words, to others and to You.

References for God's Power

1. I Kings 18:16-45

2. Matthew 6:5-15

3. James 5:13-18

Point of Truth: Yahweh is the only true God. He is all powerful and desires His creation worship Him alone.

Practical Application: How might this account of the omnipotent God affect my perception of Him and my prayer life?

24. God's Intervention

What if God showing His omnipotence and omniscience in establishing and deposing authorities such as leaders of nations, would use a Gentile king as a means of disciplining His nation by taking that nation into exile? This exile was prophesied beforehand! Then while that same king was exalting in all <u>he</u> had done and possessed, had a dream that disturbed him greatly. In seeking an interpretation of that dream by his Gentile magicians, enchanters, astrologers and diviners proved futile, it just so happened, *uh huh*, a Jewish exile had been appointed chief of the magicians. God had given him the interpretation of a dream by this same king previously, and he was now called before the king again. The interpretation was given, and the king was told that it was true. But even though he was great and prosperous, God had determined the king would be taken down, and that his mind would be reduced to that of an animal. As a result, he would eat grass and be drenched by the dew, he would live like the wild animals, his hair and nails growing unruly and this would last seven years. These events happened just as they were foretold.

Might such a display of God's foreknowledge of the events and decisions men make and the realization of how seriously God despises the sin of pride in one's life, cause us to desire to walk in humility before Him? Also, it may mean the enemy of our souls might be always tempting us to exalt ourselves, even in the smallest of matters. What an encouragement to purpose ourselves to remain humble and maintain a teachable spirit, realizing anything we know or accomplish is only through Him or by Him.

Consider all the wicked acts recorded by Nebuchadnezzar up to this event. One would think he would have continued with his wickedness after he was restored to sanity. However, he ruled a while longer and if one puts any stock into his words, it appears he may have become a believer in the One True God of Israel. Of course there is no way to know who has and has not truly been regenerated and reborn as sons of God then or today. But a tree is known by its fruit.

Sovereign Lord, grant us the necessary desire and ability to continually slay the sin of pride in our life.

24. God's Intervention/Study Guide

What if God...

1. showing His omnipotence and omniscience in establishing and deposing authorities such as leaders of nations... (Romans 13:1)

2. would use a Gentile king as a means of disciplining His nation by taking that nation into exile? This exile was prophesied beforehand! (Jeremiah 25:8-14)

3. Then while that same king was exalting in all <u>he</u> had done and possessed, he had a dream that disturbed him greatly. In seeking an interpretation of that dream through his Gentile magicians, enchanters, astrologers, and diviners, which proved futile, it just so happened, *uh huh*, a Jewish exile had been appointed chief of the magicians. God had given him the interpretation of a dream by this same king previously, and he was now called before the king again. The interpretation was given, and the king was told it was true. But even though he was great and prosperous, God had determined the king would be taken down, and that his mind would be reduced to that of an animal. As a result, he would eat grass and be drenched by the dew, he would live like the wild animals, his hair and nails would grow unruly, and this would last seven years. (Daniel 4)

4. These events happened just as they were foretold. Might such a display of God's foreknowledge of the events and decisions men make and the realization of how seriously God despises the sin of pride... (Proverbs 16:5 & 1 Peter 5:5-6)

5. in one's life cause us to desire to walk in humility before Him? (Philippians 2:3-4)

6. Also, it may mean the enemy of our souls might always be tempting us to exalt ourselves, even in the smallest of matters. (2 Corinthians 11:3)

7. What an encouragement to purpose ourselves to remain humble and maintain a teachable spirit, realizing anything we know or accomplish... (1 Corinthians 4:6-7)

8. is only through Him or by Him. (Philippians 2:13)

Sovereign Lord, grant us the necessary desire and ability to continually slay the sin of pride in our lives.

References for God's Intervention

1. Romans 13:1

2. Jeremiah 25:8-14

3. Daniel 4

4. Proverbs 16:5

   1 Peter 5:5-6

5. Philippians 2:3-4

6. 2 Corinthians 11:3

7. 1 Corinthians 4:6-7

8. Philippians 2:13

Point of Truth: God appoints all authority.

Practical Application: How does pride cause me to compromise, and how do I deal with it?

25. God's Mercy

What if God would use the illustration of a Gentile woman with a heritage of child sacrifice to show us He loves the entire world and desires that all would be saved? This particular woman was of the Canaanite people and their principle deity was Baal with a secondary deity named Asherah. The Canaanites believed Asherah was Baal's mother as well as his mistress. This belief led to immorality, religious prostitution and other wicked practices such as child sacrifice. The Canaanites were actually worshiping demons and these practices were detestable. God instructed His people to completely destroy every living being in the land of Canaan, which God had given His people as an inheritance.

But, God in His mercy being the One that created and owns all souls knew the heart of this Canaanite woman who made her living as a prostitute. Even though she grew up in the earlier-described culture and knew only what she had been taught, she had heard news of a God that had performed miraculous wonders to rescue His people from the hand of the Egyptians. By God's sovereignty and power, she believed in this wonder-working God and feared Him. Now as the Hebrew spies came to her city, under God's guiding hand, they went to her house to seek refuge and safety. Rahab welcomed them, and when the authorities of her city came to her house looking for the spies, she lied to protect them. She lied? Might we remember that God had just recently given the Law, to only His children, and she was probably ignorant of the wrong? More than likely, she had no guilt in her way of making money either, though she probably had a slight twinge of conscience, which is God's hand of love on all people. It's possible she just didn't know, but that was going to change! She asked her guest for asylum for her and her family, which they not only received, but they were also welcomed as part of God's people and she became part of the lineage of the Messiah! What an all-knowing compassionate, merciful, loving, forgiving, all powerful, sovereign Savior. He doesn't and can't change and He is just!

Consider out of all the individuals present in the land of Canaan when the Israelites began their conquest, God chose this woman to regenerate and to make part of the spiritual remnant of Israel. Not even all, and I would venture to say only a few of the Israelites were truly regenerated and part of God's spiritual people. With this in mind we have two options. We can doubt God and say He is not fair and seemingly did not give all a chance to repent or we can realize God is just and all He does is perfect and know He saves all that can justly be saved.

Merciful Savior, give us the grace to be merciful as You are and to desire justice as You do.

25. God's Mercy/Study Guide

What if God...

1. would use the illustration of a Gentile woman with a heritage of child sacrificed to show us He loves the entire world and desires that all would be saved? (Deuteronomy 12:29-31)

2. This particular woman was of the Canaanite people, and their principal deity was Baal with a secondary deity named Asherah. The Canaanites believed Asherah was Baal's mother as well as his mistress. This belief led to immorality, religious prostitution, and other wicked practices such as child sacrifice. (I Kings 14:23:24)

3. The Canaanites were actually worshiping demons... (I Corinthians 10:20)

4. and these practices were detestable. God instructed His people to completely destroy every living being in the land of Canaan, which God had given His people as an inheritance. (Deuteronomy 20:16-18)

5. But God in His mercy, being the One who created and owns all souls... (Ezekiel 18:4)

6. knew the heart of this Canaanite woman who made her living as a prostitute. Even though she grew up in the earlier-described culture and knew only what she had been taught, she had heard news of a God that had performed miraculous wonders to rescue His people from the hand of the Egyptians. By God's sovereignty and power, she believed in this wonder-working God and feared Him. Now as the Hebrew spies came to her city, under God's guiding hand, they went to her house to seek refuge and safety. Rahab welcomed them, and when the authorities of her city came to her house to look for the spies, she lied to protect them. (Joshua 2:1-13)

7. She lied? Might we remember that God had just recently given the Law, to only His children, and she was probably ignorant of the wrong. More than likely, she had no guilt in her way of making money either, though she probably had a slight twinge of conscience, which is God's hand of love on all people. (Romans 2:15)

8. It's possible that she just didn't know, but that was going to change! She asked her guests for asylum for her and her family, which they not only received, but they were also welcomed as part of God's people and she became part of the lineage of the Messiah! (Matthew 1:5)

9. What an all-knowing, compassionate, merciful, loving, forgiving, all-powerful, sovereign Savior. He doesn't and can't change... (I Samuel 15:29)

10. and He is just! (Romans 9:14 & Job 40:8)

Merciful Savior, give us the grace to be merciful as You are and to desire justice as You do.

References for God's Mercy

1. Deuteronomy 12:29-31
2. I King 14:23-24
3. I Corinthians 10:20
4. Deuteronomy 20:16-18
5. Ezekiel 18:4
6. Joshua 2:1-13
7. Romans 2:15
8. Matthew 1:5
9. I Samuel 15:29
10. Romans 9:14

Job 40:8

Point of Truth: God is full of mercy and compassion.

Practical Application: What does the enemy use from my past to cause me to doubt, and how might I overcome his lies?

26. Trusting God

What if God knows that we as His children would tend to trust those things we can see and touch, even though He tells us to be completely dependent on Him? Then, in His love, He would use a startling example to show us just how serious He is about trust. God described this man as a man after His own heart and even this man was subject, as we all are, to the influences of our enemy Satan. As believers, we can give Satan areas of our life to influence. Sadly, he completely influences the lives of the lost even if they appear good. David had committed and been forgiven of what at first glance might seem to be the most grievous sins of his life, but after this season, there seems to be an even more grievous sin than those he committed earlier. Satan influenced David to question his security as king and the strength of the nation, and also influenced him to count the men able to handle a sword in battle so he might know just how strong his fighting ability was. In doing so, he did not listen to the advice of his commander and ordered the men numbered. God, in His foreknowledge, knew all the events that were going to take place and as they unfolded this numbering of the fighting men was evil in His sight.

Consider that David was a mature and experienced man of God when Satan influenced him to sin against God here, and David completely bought into the lie. Granted the Holy Spirit of God did not and could not permanently indwell believers at this time because the atonement had not been realized. However, David was a regenerated spirit man and committed this serious sin. David's quick repentance is evident that God's spirit quickly opened His eyes to the sin but the deed was done and many suffered the consequences as we will see.

Once again, the reason for David's description as a man after God's own heart is revealed as He repented but the consequences were yet to come, as always. Seventy thousand men of Israel died, and David lived, reminding us that God's ways are above ours but He is just and we must believe and trust Him. He received very serious consequences to what might seem a harmless census. Might God in a very costly way, but a right way, be showing that sins such as murder and adultery even as serious as they are, when repented of are atoned for. But what about this trust issue? Might we begin to understand that if we do not trust Jesus (God) alone as our Savior and Lord that would mean we rely on something else? And might that mean we would be applying God-like attributes to whatever we think will help save us, be it works, place in society, our abilities, or that God is just too good to send anyone to hell? Only each individual and God would know what we are trusting in for our salvation. Jesus was crucified for applying God-like attributes to Himself and the Jews called that blasphemy. Ironically, even after Jesus' atonement, blasphemy is the only sin He said would not be forgiven.

May we trust God and God alone in His grace and compassionate mercy for our salvation!

26. Trusting God/Study Guide

What if God...

1. knows that we as His children tend to trust those things we can see and touch, even though He tells us to be completely dependent on Him? (Psalm 62:5-6)

2. Then, in His love, He would use a startling example to show us just how serious He is about trust. God described this man as a man after His own heart... (I Samuel 13:14)

3. and even this man was subject, as we all are, to the influences of our enemy, Satan. As believers, we can give Satan areas of our life to influence. (Ephesians 4:26-27)

4. Sadly, he completely influences the lives of the lost even if they appear good. (Romans 8:6-8)

5. David had committed and been forgiven of what at first glance might seem to be the most grievous sins of his life... (2 Samuel 11)

6. but after this season, there seems to be an even more grievous sin than those he committed earlier. Satan influenced David to question his security as king and the nation and influenced him to count the men able to handle a sword in battle so he might know just how strong his fighting ability was. In doing so, he did not listen to the advice of his commander and ordered the men numbered. God, in His foreknowledge, knew all the events that were going to take place, and as they unfolded, this numbering of the fighting men was evil in His sight. (I Chronicles 21)

7. Once again, the reason for David's description as a man after God's own heart is revealed as He repented, but the consequences were yet to come, as always. Seventy thousand men of Israel died, and David lived, reminding us that God's ways are above ours, but He

is just and we must believe and trust Him. He received very serious consequences to what might seem a harmless census. Might God in a very costly way, but in a right way... (Psalm 19:9)

8. be showing that sins such as murder and adultery, even as serious as they are, when repented of, are atoned for? (1 John 2:2)

9. But what about this trust issue? (Proverbs 3:5-6)

10. Might we begin to understand that if we do not trust Jesus (God) alone as our Savior and Lord... (Ephesians 2:8-9)

11. that would mean we rely on something else? And might that mean we are applying God-like attributes to whatever we think will help save us, be it works, place in society, our abilities, or the idea that God is just too good to send anyone to hell? Only each individual and God would know what we are trusting in for our salvation. Jesus was crucified for applying God-like attributes to Himself... (Mark 14:62-64)

12. and the Jews called that blasphemy. Ironically, even after Jesus' atonement, blasphemy is the only sin He said would not be forgiven. (Mark 3:28-29)

May we trust God and God alone in His grace and compassionate mercy for our salvation!

References for Trusting God

1. Psalm 62:5-6

2. 1 Samuel 13:14

3. Ephesians 4:26-27

4. Romans 8:6-8

5. 2 Samuel 11

6. 1 Chronicles 21

7. Psalm 19:9

8. 1 John 2:2

9. Proverbs 3:5-6

10. Ephesians 2:8-9

11. Mark 14:62-64

12. Mark 3:28-29

Point of Truth: Trusting God alone in every matter of our lives is essential to honoring Him.

Practical Application: What am I tempted to trust other than God and what part of my life does that affect?

27. Standing Alone

What if God knew there would be times all those who truly follow Him as we travel through an alien land would be required to stand alone? Just what does it take for a young person that is under the stress of peer pressure or an older person or for that matter any of us that are believers, to have the boldness to stand alone, regardless of the cost? We might be reminded of two bold men as Moses led the Hebrew people to the Promised Land. These two were chosen with ten others to go into Canaan and spy out the land. While the courage of ten men failed them at the sight of the men occupying the land, two men, Joshua and Caleb, believed God and were bold enough to face even the possibility of being stoned. Once again a severe price was paid for disobedience and the effect was endured even by the innocent as that entire generation was prohibited from entering the Promised Land, except for those two bold men Joshua and Caleb. They were delayed forty years before their faith was realized.

Consider the last time you were put in a compromising situation. Were you satisfied with your response and did you stand for what was right or is there a possibility you blinked and that has concerned you since it happened. We all struggle and prayerfully by God's empowerment the next time you will stand for what is right!

One essential element to standing alone is the confidence in what you are standing for is right, and might that be the birthplace of boldness? A militant determined to commit an act of terror is bold enough to give his own life because he believes he is right. Might we, as believers in God and his Word, be confident enough to obey His Word at any cost knowing that our reward is far greater than the cost? On the other hand, might the cost of compromise and disobedience be much greater than we might anticipate and even put into question if we are authentic believers? Standing alone is never easy, and we can be assured there will be a price to pay, but knowing we will be empowered to stand certainly will increase our confidence because His Word is trustworthy. Jehovah Jireh (Provider) will provide if we acknowledge our complete dependence on Him.

Jehovah Jireh, as we depend on You for protection and courage increase our boldness and desire to be obedient to You as You allow trials and tests for our good.

27. Standing Alone/Study Guide

What if God...

1. knew there would be times all those who truly follow Him as we travel through an alien land would be required to stand alone? Just what does it take for a young person under the stress of peer pressure, an older person, or for that matter any of us who are believers, to have the boldness to stand alone, regardless of the cost?

    We might be reminded of two bold men as Moses led the Hebrew people to the Promised Land. These two were chosen with ten others to go into Canaan and spy out the land. While the courage of ten men failed them at the sight of those occupying the land, two men, Joshua and Caleb, believed God and were bold enough to face even the possibility of being stoned. (Numbers 13:26-33 & 14:1-10)

2. Once again a severe price was paid for disobedience and the effect was endured even by the innocent as that entire generation was prohibited from entering the Promised Land, except for those two bold men, Joshua and Caleb. (Numbers 14:26-30)

3. They were delayed forty years... (Numbers 14:34)

4. before their faith was realized. One essential element to standing alone is the confidence in what you are standing for is right, and might that be the birthplace of boldness? (Proverbs 28:1 & 2 Corinthians 3:12 NIV)

5. A militant determined to commit an act of terror is bold enough to give his own life because he believes he is right. Might we, as believers in God and His Word, be confident enough to obey that Word... (John 14:23-24)

6. at any cost, knowing our reward is far greater than the cost? (Matthew 5:12)

7. On the other hand, might the cost of compromise and disobedience be much greater than we might anticipate, and even put into question, if we are authentic believers? (I John 3:6)

8. Standing alone is never easy, and we can be assured there will be a price to pay... (I Peter 3:17)

9. but knowing we will be empowered to stand certainly will increase our confidence because His Word is trustworthy. (John 17:17)

10. Jehovah Jireh (Provider) will provide if we acknowledge our complete dependence on Him. (Genesis 22:14)

Jehovah Jireh, as we depend on You for protection and courage, increase our boldness and desire to be obedient to You as You allow trials and tests for our good.

References for Standing Alone

1. Numbers 13:26-33

    Numbers 14:1-10

2. Numbers 14:26-30

3. Numbers 14:34

4. Proverbs 28:1

    2 Corinthians 3:12 1984 (NIV)

5. John 14:23-24

6. Matthew 5:12

7. 1 John 3:6

8. 1 Peter 3:17

9. John 17:17

10. Genesis 22:14

Point of Truth: Not compromising God's truth is part of an obedient life.

Practical Application: How have I stood alone on God's truth and where could I use strengthening?

CHAPTER SEVEN
PERSON AND WORK OF JESUS

28. Jesus

What if God willed in His sovereignty, at just the right time in history to have His Holy Spirit visit a humble virgin, and with that visit, the young woman would find herself with child? Having been previously visited by a supernatural being named Gabriel, she was informed of the events that would take place. Because she was a virgin and the Seed implanted was truly holy, the child she would carry was called the Holy One. This child would have the very nature of God. He is God! This child would grow and be perfectly obedient through suffering and again, when the time was just right would be baptized by his cousin, John, and minister by healing the blind, lame, those with leprosy, and the deaf, and even raise the dead to life. He preached good news to the poor and blessed all that did not fall away because of Him. Then after only three short years of ministry, God, knowing the severity of capital punishment in that day, was pleased to have Him stricken, His beard torn from His cheeks, spat upon and mocked, His appearance so disfigured beyond that of any man and His form marred beyond human likeness. This Holy One set His face like a flint to accomplish all the Father had willed and with that He is the only way to the Father.

Consider a man so kind and loving that you are unusually drawn to Him. The words He speaks are firm but seem to brim with an element of hope and they speak of freedom and encouragement. He speaks only the truth and when He is talking to the leaders and teachers that you have trusted, but for some reason not completely, He seems to speak with exceptional harshness. What He says is new and fresh and He speaks of a kingdom where everything is right and just. Then as suddenly as He came on the scene, He is gone. Crucified in the harshest way and all that is left is emptiness, silence and a fearful expectation of the future. Then suddenly He is back again full of life and speaking of peace and giving you a purpose to go and encourage others to follow and be His disciples also. But now, after He met with you, what He says is clearer and makes sense and thinking back over the last three years there was so much that was confusing that now seems to be fitting into place. And He has said all along that He is leaving again, very soon, but He will still be available to you and somehow you know what He says is true.

We might find ourselves questioning whether all this was necessary; but we also might realize that it took His blood, death and resurrection to pay the price of atoning for the sin of the entire world. The atonement takes away every sin, save that of blasphemy (assigning to oneself the attributes of God) that Jesus declared would not be forgiven, and is it possible that very sin will doom all those who do not believe as they will attempt to save themselves at the Great White Throne judgment. Might we be truly humbled when we realize His ways are not our ways and His thoughts are so much higher than any man's?

Thank you, Jesus for Your unspeakable gift and for paying the enormous price to atone for the sin of the world.

Chapter Seven
Person and Work of Jesus

28. Jesus/Study Guide

What if God...

1. willed in His sovereignty, at just the right time... (Ecclesiastes 3:17; Romans 5:6)

2. in history to have His Holy Spirit visit a humble virgin, and with that visit, the young woman would find herself with child? Having been previously visited by a supernatural being named Gabriel, she was informed of the events that would take place. Because she was a virgin and the Seed implanted was truly holy, the child she would carry was called the Holy One. (Luke 1:26-38)

3. This child would have the very nature of God. He is God! (John 10:30)

4. This child would grow and become perfectly obedient through suffering... (Hebrews 5:8-9)

5. and again, when the time was just right, He would be baptized by his cousin, John... (Matthew 3:13-16)

6. and minister by healing the blind, the lame, the leprous, and the deaf, and even raise the dead to life. He preached the good news to the poor and blessed all that did not fall away because of Him. (Matthew 11:5-6)

7. Then after only three short years of ministry, God, knowing the severity of capital punishment in that day, was pleased to have Him stricken... (Isaiah 53)

8. His beard torn from His cheeks, spat upon and mocked, His appearance so disfigured beyond that of any man, and His form marred beyond human likeness. This Holy One set His face like a flint... (Isaiah 52:14 & 50:6-7)

9. to accomplish all the Father had willed... (John 17:4)

10. and with that He is the only way to the Father. (John 14:6)

11. We might find ourselves questioning whether all this was necessary, but we also might realize it took His blood, death, and resurrection to pay the price of atoning for the sin of the entire world. (I John 2:2)

12. The atonement takes away every sin, save that of blasphemy... (Mark 3:28-29)

13. (assigning to oneself the attributes of God) ... (Numbers 15:30-31: See dictionary. reference.com)

14. that Jesus declared would not be forgiven, and is it possible that very sin will doom all those who do not believe, as they will attempt to save themselves at the Great White Throne judgment. (Revelation 20:11-15)

15. Might we be truly humbled when we realize His ways are not our ways and His thoughts are so much higher than any man's? (Isaiah 55:8-9)

Thank you, Jesus, for Your unspeakable gift and for paying the enormous price to atone for the sin of the world.

References for Jesus

1. Ecclesiastes 3:17

    Romans 5:6

2. Luke 1:26-38

3. John 10:30

4. Hebrews 5:8-9

5. Matthew 3:13-16

6. Matthew 11:5-6

7. Isaiah 53

8. Isaiah 52:14

    Isaiah 50:6-7

9. John 17:4

10. John 14:6

11. 1 John 2:2

12. Mark 3:28-29

13. Numbers 15:30-31

14. Revelation 20:11-15

15. Isaiah 55:8-9

Point of Truth: Jesus is the atoning sacrifice for the sins of the whole world. The curtain separating us from God's holiness is torn apart, and the price (sacrifice) is paid and completed. Ownership has changed if you are a true believer.

Practical Application: How do the Messiah's death and the atoning of sin affect my life and my relationship to God?

29. Sin's Defeat

What if God in his almighty power so permanently dealt with sin when He died on the cross that as His spirit left His body, the curtain that separated the Holy of Holies from the remainder of the temple was torn from top to bottom? God ordained this place, this Holy of Holies to be separated or set apart, and the only one who could pass through the veil was the High Priest once a year on the Day of Atonement. On this day, blood sacrifices were made in strict obedience to God's commands to atone for the sin of all the nation of Israel, the priest, and the people. If any sinfulness were to enter the Holy of Holies the possessor of that sin would be consumed by God's holiness and destroyed. Centuries of blood sacrifices had been made in this sacred place, first in the portable tabernacle, then the temple Solomon built; and finally, at the end of the seventy-year exile, this Holy of Holies was built and stood as Jesus lived, ministered, and was crucified. It was here the veil, or curtain, was torn from top to bottom as God's hand accepted Jesus' blood sacrifice as the final payment and the sins of the world were permanently atoned for. No other sacrifice would ever be necessary! It was finished!

Consider that sin (the world, flesh and the devil) had dominated and held captive all of human kind since the fall and there was no known escape until Jesus' crucifixion. Until then, as now, only those God supernaturally regenerated truly sought Him and had a relationship with Him but the difficulty of sin still dominated. Even today we see that sin is prevalent, however, God is, on His timetable, purposefully gathering all His people through the obedient witness of His people, visions, dreams and by the clear message His creation speaks and He will not overlook any. Sin has now been defanged for all that believe on Jesus, though it is still a menace and must be dealt with as we will see in the following chapters. But in Jesus Christ, the captives of sin have been set free.

One of Jesus' first destinations after His death was to Sheol, the holding place for the dead--all the dead--righteous and wicked. More than likely a great chasm separated one from the other, and while Jesus was there, He preached to the captives that He was the One that had been prophesied and that they had longed for, but now with the price paid, He released all the elect of all past ages from their captivity and led them with Him to paradise, where the thief who believed in Him on the cross had been escorted by angels to his new home. Sin has now lost its ownership of all the souls who will believe on Jesus, and receive Him as Savior and Lord of their life. They have been set free from the power of death, the grave and sin. We are now truly free to be bound to righteousness!

Worthy Lamb of God, all praise, honor and power unto You, give us grace to walk obediently in our freedom.

29. Sin's Defeat/Study Guide

What if God, in His almighty power...

1. so permanently dealt with sin when He died on the cross that as His spirit left His body, the curtain that separated the Holy of Holies from the remainder of the temple was torn from top to bottom? (Mark 15:38)

2. God ordained this place, this Holy of Holies, to be separated or set apart, and the only one who could pass through the veil was the High Priest once a year on the day of atonement. On this day, blood sacrifices were made in strict obedience to God's commands to atone for the sin of all the nation of Israel, the priest, and the people. If any sinfulness were to enter the Holy of Holies, the possessor of that sin would be consumed by God's holiness and destroyed.

   Centuries of blood sacrifices have been made in this sacred place, first in the portable tabernacle; then in the temple Solomon built; and finally, at the end of the seventy-year exile, this Holy of Holies was built and stood as Jesus lived, ministered, and was crucified. It was here the veil, or curtain, was torn from top to bottom because God's hand accepted Jesus' blood sacrifice as the final payment, and the sins of the world were permanently atoned for. No other sacrifice would ever be necessary! It was finished! One of Jesus' first destinations after His death, was to Sheol, the holding place for the dead -- all the dead -- the righteous and the wicked. (Psalm 89:48)

3. More than likely a great chasm separated one from the other... (Luke 16:26)

4. and while Jesus was there, He preached to the captives that He was the One... (I Peter 3:18-19 & 4:6)

5. who had been prophesied and that they had longed for, but now with the price paid, He released all the elect of all the past ages from their captivity and led them with Him... (Ephesians 4:8-10)

6. to paradise, where the thief who believed in Him on the cross... (Luke 23:40-43)

7. had been escorted by angels to his new home. (Luke 16:22)

8. Sin has now lost its ownership... (Romans 6:6-7)

9. of all the souls who will believe on Jesus and receive Him as Savior and Lord of their lives. They have been set free from the power of death, the grave, and sin. We are now truly free to be bound to righteousness! (Romans 6:18)

Worthy Lamb of God, all praise, honor, and power unto You, give us grace to walk obediently in our freedom.

References for Sin's Defeat

1. Mark 15:38

2. Psalm 89:48

3. Luke 16:26

4. I Peter 3:18-19

    I Peter 4:6

5. Ephesians 4:8-10

6. Luke 23:40-43

7. Luke 16:22

8. Romans 6:6-7

9. Romans 6:18

Point of Truth: Sin, death, and the grave have lost their hold on all who will turn to Jesus as Savior and Lord.

Practical Application: Knowing that sin is a defeated foe, how might I walk in obedience to Jesus' commands, knowing He said, "If you love me you will obey my commands"?

30. Jewish Feast / Jesus

What if God desiring to show His foreknowledge of all events and His Almighty power would institute the Jewish festivals with His coming as Messiah in mind?

In ordaining the Passover Feast; the lamb was prepared, an unblemished sacrifice was made at twilight. The blood, being spilled, and spread over the lintel and doorpost to save His people from death. Jesus, the perfect Lamb, crucified on Passover, which began on Friday that same day. He spilled His perfect blood to save all men and women, who believe on Him and make Him Lord, from certain death.

The Feast of Unleavened Bread; as unleavened bread is considered pure, Jesus the pure (sinless) bread of life had been buried in a borrowed tomb and was in the earth during this feast on the Sabbath.

The Feast of First Fruits followed the Sunday after The Feast of Unleavened Bread and was instituted to bring the first of the grain harvest to the priest. It is significant that our Savior rose from the dead in the early morning on this day as He is the first fruits of all those that will be raised at the resurrection.

The Feast of Weeks; from the Sunday that First Fruits occurred the Jews counted 50 days and began the Feast of Weeks (Pentecost). On that day the church was born with the indwelling of the Holy Spirit.

Thus the spring feast concluded and the next feast, as with the church is the Feast of Trumpets. This was the beginning of the fall feast, which was commemorated with a trumpet blast and ended with the Day of Atonement, the high and holy day in which the high priest entered the Holy of Holies to seek atonement for the sins of the people. The church associates the trumpet blast with the rapture and the consummation of the church realizing its atonement and the initiation of soon coming 1000-year reign of Messiah on earth in which the Feast of Tabernacles will be celebrated every year in Jerusalem.

Thus fulfilling the original feast ordained by God. Coincidence, probably not. What an Almighty, All-knowing, Ever-present (Transcendent), Unchanging (Perfect) God we serve. And this Sovereign God loves His people, Jew and Gentile, in a different way than he loves the world. Sadly, He will pour out His wrath upon all those that will not turn to Him in repentance and believe. And in His sovereignty, He knows both the redeemed and the unredeemed, even before they are born!

Consider the beauty of this portrait God the Father painted of Jesus the Son through these original Jewish feast and his relationship with His bride in waiting and their future together.

Eternal Father, You are wise beyond our understanding and may we celebrate You in Your greatness.

30. Jewish Feast(Jesus) /Study Guide

What if God, desiring to show His foreknowledge of all events and His Almighty power...

1. would institute the Jewish festivals with His coming as Messiah in mind? In ordaining the Passover Feast, the lamb was prepared and an unblemished sacrifice was made at twilight. The blood was spilled and spread over the lintel and doorpost to save His people from death. (Leviticus 23:4-5)

2. Jesus, the perfect Lamb, was crucified on Passover, which began on Friday that same day. He spilled His perfect blood to save all men and women... (Revelation 5:9)

3. who believe on Him and make Him Lord... (I John 3:4-6)

4. from certain death. As unleavened bread is considered pure, Jesus, the pure (sinless) bread of life... (Leviticus 23:6-8)

5. had been buried in a borrowed tomb and was in the earth during the Feast of Unleavened Bread on the Sabbath. (Luke 23:50-55)

6. The Feast of First Fruits followed the Sunday after the Feast of Unleavened Bread and was instituted to bring the first of the grain harvest to the priest. (Leviticus 23:9-14)

7. It is significant that our Savior rose in the early morning on this day... (Luke 24:1-12)

8. as He is the first fruits of all those who will be raised at the resurrection. (ICorinthians 15:20)

9. From the Sunday that First Fruits occurred, the Jews counted fifty days and began the Feast of Weeks (Pentecost). (Leviticus 23:15-22)

10. On that day, the church was born with the indwelling of the Holy Spirit. (Acts 2:1-4)

11. Thus the spring feast concluded and the next feast, as with the church, is the Feast of Trumpets. This was the beginning of the fall feast, which was commemorated with a trumpet blast and ended with the Day of Atonement, the high and holy day in which the high priest entered the Holy of Holies to seek atonement for the sins of the people. (Leviticus 23:23-32)

12. The church associates the trumpet blast with the rapture, the consummation of the church realizing its atonement... (I Thessalonians 4:13-18)

13. and the initiation of the soon-coming thousand-year reign of the Messiah on earth... (Revelation 20:1-6)

14. in which the Feast of the Tabernacles will be celebrated every year in Jerusalem... (Zechariah 14:16-19)

15. thus fulfilling the original feast that God ordained. Coincidence? Probably not. What an Almighty, all-knowing, ever-present (transcendent), unchanging (perfect) God we serve. And this sovereign God loves His people, Jew and Gentile, in a different way than he loves the world. Sadly, He will pour out His wrath upon all those who will not turn to Him in repentance and believe. (Romans 2:5)

16. And in His sovereignty, He knows both the redeemed and the unredeemed, even before they are born! (Romans 9:11)

Eternal Father, You are wise beyond our understanding, and may we celebrate You in Your greatness.

References for Jewish Feast/Jesus

1. Leviticus 23:4-5
2. Revelation 5:9
3. I John 3:4-6
4. Leviticus 23:6-8
5. Luke 23:50-55
6. Leviticus 23:9-14
7. Luke 24:1-12
8. I Corinthians 15:20
9. Leviticus 23:15-22
10. Acts 2:1-4
11. Leviticus 23:23-32
12. I Thessalonians 4:13-18
13. Revelation 20:1-6
14. Zechariah 14:16-19
15. Romans 2:5
16. Romans 9:11

Point of Truth: Jesus is the Jewish Messiah, and we should never forget the Jewishness of our Christian faith.

Practical Application: Does this give you a fresh perspective of God's ordained feast and what might that be?

31. Sign of Jonah

What if God in showing His omnipresence and omniscience of future events would speak of the sign of Jonah in somewhat of a mysterious way to some of the Pharisees and teachers of the Law? In one way, God told the Assyrians (Ninevites) of Jonah's day that they would be destroyed if they did not repent. He, in the same way, told the Pharisee's and teachers of the Law of their fate if they did not repent. Part of the sign they would be given is that as Jonah was in the belly of the fish, so Jesus would be in the earth after His death. But even as Jonah was returned to life when the fish spewed him out on the land, Jesus life was returned to His body that had died and He was resurrected assuring salvation for all that believe. Most of these Jews would be witnesses of these events that were soon to happen, but most would not believe and repent. The Assyrians did, however, repent and were spared, eventually being used by God to punish the northern ten tribes of Israel, who were exiled from their homeland.

That being said in Jesus day, the same call now goes out to our obstinate culture to repent as people are aborting (murdering) babies, calling evil good by embracing and legalizing so-called same-sex marriage, parents are obeying their children and the list goes on. The cry "Righteousness exalts a nation, but sin is a disgrace to any people" goes out.

But how is this a "sign of Jonah" today? Might we look back to September 11, 2001 and remember many of those that attacked our nation were of Assyrian heritage (regions of Iraq, Saudi Arabia, Iran and Turkey), as we defiantly say with pride and arrogance of heart, "The bricks have fallen down, but we will replace them with dressed stone; the fig trees have been felled, but we will replace them with cedars." Having said this, by continually rebelling and engaging in sinful activities, we are thereby giving lip service to God and telling Him we don't want or need His help, just as the Israelites did in their day. With such events still fresh in our minds might we realize the possibility that we are in the season that is prophesied as the "day of our Lord" and the coming great tribulation may not be far away as God's judgment and wrath begin to be poured out on the earth? Might that mean the sign of Jonah is a call to repentance or certain destruction will follow?

Consider the seriousness of the day we live in and people still go on in their wickedness, buying and selling, marrying and giving in marriage as if there is no responsibility as to our lives. But God in His mercy is still saving and regenerating His elect as they hear the call. Let's be diligent in proclaiming the call.

Holy God, You are longsuffering and forbearing, grant that we will walk in repentance and help our unbelief.

31. The Sign of Jonah/Study Guide

What if God, in showing His omnipresence and omniscience of future events...

1. would speak of the sign of Jonah in somewhat of a mysterious way to some of the Pharisees and teachers of the Law? (Matthew 12:38-40)

2. In one way, God told the Assyrians (Ninevites) of Jonah's day that they would be destroyed if they did not repent. (Jonah 3)

3. He, in the same way, told the Pharisees and teachers of the Law of their fate if they did not repent. Part of the sign they would be given is that as Jonah was in the belly of the fish, so Jesus would be in the earth after His death. But even as Jonah was returned to life when the fish spewed him out on land, Jesus' life was returned to His body that had died and He was resurrected, assuring salvation for all who believe. Most of these Jews would be witnesses of these events that were soon to happen, but most would not believe and repent. (Matthew 12:41)

4. The Assyrians did, however, repent and were spared, and God eventually used them to punish the northern ten tribes of Israel, who were exiled from their homeland. (Isaiah 10:5-6)

5. That being said in Jesus' day, the same call now goes out to our obstinate culture to repent as people are aborting (murdering) babies and calling evil good by embracing and legalizing so-called same-sex marriage, parents are obeying their children, and the list goes on. (2 Timothy 3:1-5)

6. The cry, "Righteousness exalts a nation, but sin is a disgrace to any people" goes out. (Proverbs 14:34)

7. But how is this a "sign of Jonah" today? Might we look back at September 11, 2001, and remember that many of those who attacked our nation were Assyrians (Iraqis), as we defiantly say with pride and arrogance of heart, "The bricks have fallen down, but we will replace them with dressed stone; the fig trees have been felled, but we will replace them with cedars." (Isaiah 9:10; See www.youtube.com Tom Daschle, September 12, 2001)

8. Having said this, by continually rebelling and engaging in sinful activities, we are thereby giving lip service to God and telling Him that we don't want or need His help, just as the Israelites did in their day. With such events still fresh in our minds, might we realize the possibility that we are in the season prophesied as the "day of our Lord" and the coming tribulation may not be far away, as God's judgment and wrath begin to be poured out on the earth? Might that mean the sign of Jonah is a call to repentance or certain destruction will follow? (Matthew 24:32-34)

Holy God, You are longsuffering and forbearing. Grant that we will walk in repentance, and help our unbelief.

References for the Sign of Jonah

1. Matthew 12:38-40

2. Jonah 3

3. Matthew 12:41

4. Isaiah 10:5-6

5. 2 Timothy 3:1-5

6. Proverbs 14:34 NIV

7. Isaiah 9:10

    YouTube / Tom Daschle, September 12, 2001

8. Matthew 24:32-34

Point of Truth: Believing with a repentant heart and walking in a lifestyle of repentance is the only way to escape God's coming wrath.

Practical Application: How might I have compromised my walk with God to fit into cultural norms and worldly thinking?

32. Parables

What if God in speaking to the crowds in parables would explain how our and God's enemy would corrupt the kingdom work of building the church, thereby making the kingdom appear larger than it really is? In the parable of the sower it seems likely that only one of the seeds (possibly two) are true believers. We will hold to one since those that find the narrow gate are few. The other seeds are taken away, withered, or were choked thus bearing no fruit.

Then in the parable of the weeds, the enemy sowed weeds among the good seed, and they grew together until the harvest when the angels separated the two and the weeds were destroyed.

Now the mustard seed which normally produces a plant abnormally becomes a tree. Then birds, possibly the same ones that ate up the seeds the farmer allowed to fall along the path in the parable of the sower; perch in the tree produced by the mustard seed, but are not really part of the kingdom.

Then when the woman mixed yeast into the large amount of flour and worked it though out the dough, the loaf became larger than an unleavened or pure loaf. Yeast here, as always, representing sin or the work of the devil.

Then there are two parables that speak of the great value of the kingdom when discovered and though there is a cost, possibly even a great cost, there was no hesitation in paying the price.

With one more parable He wanted the people to hear, Jesus spoke of a net let down into the lake, in which all kinds of fish are caught. Once again the angels separate the wicked from the righteous.

Consider today, we are in an environment of seeker friendly churches and many are hesitant to preach the necessity of walking in obedience to God's word. Jesus made it clear, "If you love me, you will obey what I command." (John 14:15) NIV. Also He said that a tree is known by its fruit and a good tree bears good fruit and a bad tree bears bad fruit. The sobering words He spoke are that He never knew those that do not do the Father's will.

Might we also find such a fascinating teaching sobering, as we ponder it, and are motivated to make our calling and election sure. We, realizing the gravity of such truth, might desire to work out our salvation with fear and trembling, which is our responsibility, but how encouraging to realize it is God who works in you to will and to act according to His good purpose, His sovereignty. That's a great balance of our responsibility and God's sovereignty!

Father God, enable us to walk confidently that we are Yours because we see the fruit of Your Spirit at work in our lives.

32. Parables/Study Guide

What if God, in speaking to the crowds in parables...

1. would explain how our and God's enemy would corrupt the kingdom work of building the church, thereby making the kingdom appear larger than it really is? In the parable of the sower, it seems likely that only one of the seeds mentioned (possibly two) are the true believers. We will hold to one, however, since those who find the narrow gate are few. (Matthew 7:13)

2. The other seeds are taken away, withered, or were choked, thus bearing no fruit. (Matthew 13:1-23)

3. Then in the parable of the weeds, the enemy sowed weeds among the good seed, and they grew together until the harvest when the angels separated the two and the weeds were destroyed. (Matthew 13:24-30)

4. Now the mustard seed, which normally produces a plant, abnormally becomes a tree. Then birds, possibly the same ones that ate the seeds the farmer allowed to fall along the path in the parable of the sower, perch in the tree produced by the mustard seed, but are not really part of the kingdom. (Matthew 13:31-32)

5. Then when the woman mixed yeast into the large amount of flour and worked it throughout the dough, the loaf became larger than an unleavened, or pure, loaf. Yeast here, as always, represents sin or the work of the devil. (Matthew 13:33-35)

6. Then there are two parables that speak of the great value of the kingdom when discovered, and though there is a cost, possibly even a great cost, there is no hesitation in paying the price. (Matthew 13:44-45)

7. With one more parable that He wanted the people to hear, Jesus spoke of a net let down into the lake, in which all kinds of fish are caught. Once again, the angels separate the wicked from the righteous. (Matthew 13:47-50)

8. Might we also find such a fascinating teaching sobering, as we ponder it, and make our calling and election sure? (2 Peter 1:5-11)

9. We, realizing the gravity of such truth, might desire to work out our salvation with fear and trembling, which is our responsibility, but how encouraging it is to realize that God works in you to will and to act according to His good purpose, His sovereignty. That's a great balance of our responsibility and God's sovereignty! (Philippians 2:12-13)

Father God, enable us to walk confidently that we are Yours because we see the fruit of Your Spirit at work in our lives.

References for Parables

1. Matthew 7:13

2. Matthew 13:1-23

3. Matthew 13:24-30

4. Matthew 13:31-32

5. Matthew 13:33-35

6. Matthew 13:44-45

7. Matthew 13:47-50

8. 2 Peter 1:5-11

9. Philippians 2:12-13

Point of Truth: We must grow and mature, even as there is worldliness on every side.

Practical Application: How do I make my calling and election sure?

33. Contemporary Pharisees

What if God while He dwelt among us in the flesh purposed in His severe proclamation against the Pharisees and the teachers of the Law would show us a wonderfully simple truth that would apply to all men for all time? It did seem that Jesus was constantly harassed by the earlier-mentioned group at many different events and much of that harassment was due to the fact He contradicted their teaching about the Sabbath and His miracles. As history records, this same group had killed many prophets, wise men and teachers, but was it the self-righteousness and condescending attitude of members of this group that destined them to destruction? Was it even their pride, when they sought to be noticed, or their piety that doomed them? How about their seemingly endless additions to the Law of God that placed all sorts of burdens on men's backs, or the hypocrisy that seemed to run rampant among them? The list of woes that Jesus spoke against these men is lengthy indeed but there was one simple truth they could not see!

Consider the human condition is as it has been since the fall, and with such a depraved condition in mankind's captivity to Satan, no one can hear the call to believe and repent due to that captivity. One may hear the words to repent and believe in Jesus, however, the call is heard with flesh ears and the need is not recognized. Only God can, by His power, bring one dead in trespasses and sin to life and regenerate their heart, thus enabling them to hear the call with spiritual ears and that call will be effective and lead to saving faith, belief in Jesus and repentance.

Is it possible that there are Pharisees among us today in the church, and what might a modern-day Pharisee look like? Jesus spoke of another situation that may give us a clue to how a modern-day Pharisee may manifest. Might we, in a situation where a brother or sister sins against us, in obedience and love, go to that brother or sister, one on one, in hopes of repentance and reconciliation. Then if he or she refuses, in obedience we take one or two others. If that person still refuses to repent, in obedience and love, we bring the situation before the church. If at this point, the person still refuses to repent, does it appear that we are to treat him or her as if he or she is not truly part of the church? What about all those in the church who may hear a sermon or teaching and know they may be guilty of certain sins mentioned but still refuse to repent?

Jesus atoned for all the sins He listed against the Pharisees and the only requirement is to believe and repent, but Jesus said of the Pharisees and others, because He knew their hearts, you refuse to come to Me to have life. It is encouraging to know that some in that day, such as Nicodemus, did believe and repented, as well as Joseph of Arimathea, who provided Jesus' tomb. Not to mention Saul who became Paul and was God's tool to take the gospel to the Gentiles. As in Jonah's day the cry goes out to repent or be destroyed and in Jesus' day the same sign of Jonah given, repent or be destroyed. And today, the cry, simply believe and repent or be destroyed, goes out to all!

Gracious Lord, give us ears to hear and eyes to see that we may truly believe and walk in repentance.

33. Contemporary Pharisees/Study Guide

What if God, while He dwelt among us in the flesh...

1. purposed in His severe proclamation against the Pharisees and the teachers of the Law to show us a wonderfully simple truth that would apply to all men for all time? It did seem that Jesus was constantly harassed by the earlier-mentioned group at many different events... (John 5:16-17)

2. and much of that harassment was due to the fact that He contradicted their teaching about the Sabbath and His miracles. (John 9:16)

3. As history records, this same group had killed many prophets, wise men, and teachers... (Matthew 23:34)

4. but was it the self-righteousness and condescending attitude of members of this group that destined them to destruction? Was it even their pride, when they sought to be noticed, or their piety that doomed them? How about their seemingly endless additions to the Law of God that placed all sorts of burdens on men's backs, or the hypocrisy that seemed to run rampant amongst them? The list of woes that Jesus spoke against these men is lengthy indeed... (Matthew 23:1-33)

5. but there was one simple truth they could not see! Is it possible that there are Pharisees among us today in the church, and what might a modern Pharisee look like? Jesus spoke of another situation that may give us a clue to how a modern-day Pharisee may manifest. Might we, in a situation where a brother or sister sins against us, in obedience and love, go to that brother or sister, one on one, in hopes of repentance and reconciliation? Then, if he or she refuses, and in obedience, we take one or two others. If the person still refuses to repent, in obedience and love, we then bring the situation before the church. If at this point, the person still refuses to repent, does

it appear that we are to treat him or her as if he or she is not truly part of the church? (Matthew 18:15-19)

6. What about all those in the church who hear a sermon or teaching and know they may be guilty of certain sins mentioned, but still refuse to repent? Jesus atoned for all the sins He listed against the Pharisees... (I Peter 3:18)

7. and the only requirement is to believe and repent, but Jesus said of the Pharisees and others, because He knew their hearts, they refused to come to Him to have life. (John 5:40)

8. It is encouraging to know that some in that day, such as Nicodemus, did believe and repented... (John 19:39)

9. as well as Joseph of Arimathea, who provided Jesus' tomb. (John 19:38)

10. Not to mention Saul who became Paul... (Acts 9)

11. and was God's tool to take the Gospel to the Gentiles. (Romans 15:15-16)

12. As in Jonah's day, the cry goes out to repent or be destroyed... (Jonah 3:1-10)

13. and in Jesus' day the same sign of Jonah, repent or be destroyed, is given. And today, the cry, simply believe and repent or be destroyed, goes out to all! (Acts 2:38-39 & Romans 6:23)

Gracious Lord, give us ears to hear and eyes to see that we may truly walk in repentance and believe.

References for Contemporary Pharisees

1. John 5:16-17

2. John 9:16

3. Matthew 23:24

4. Matthew 23:1-33

5. Matthew 18:15-19

6. 1 Peter 3:18

7. John 5:40

8. John 19:39

9. John 19:38

10. Acts 9

11. Romans 15:15-16

12. Jonah 3:1-10

    Acts 2:38-39

13. Romans 6:23

Point of Truth: Believe that Jesus the Messiah of Israel is the only way to the Father. Repent of your sin and you will be saved. Walk in repentance.

Practical Application: Do I have difficulty repenting of certain sins?

CHAPTER EIGHT
Christian Life / Man's Responsibility

34. Believer's Freedom

What if God, the only all-powerful, all-knowing being, knowing His Son's death on the cross and resurrection back to life, displayed His power and completely secured freedom and redemption, so that now anything is permissible for believers? **Hold on there!** Now we can just do anything? What might that mean? Oh, there's more, but not everything is beneficial. But, what if I'm willing to take that risk? Well maybe, my old master is still in the hunt, not for my soul but to destroy some part of me, or maybe me altogether, and he might make certain activities or old habits so alluring that I really want to get involved in them again. It certainly can be tempting because part of me received much pleasure from that old way of life, but in all honesty, those consequences always brought shame, pain and just a big mess that needed cleaning up. Sometimes scars were left that are still with me. Maybe those scars are a good reminder when something, sweet and tender says, "This is not a good idea" and as we resist the temptation, are strangely empowered to turn away from the allurement. Might that sweet tender voice be the Holy Spirit that now indwells us and if we find ourselves dwelling on and embracing the temptation His voice is less and less noticeable?

Consider the season in your life when God's work of transformation brought you to the point that the besetting sin that so easily caused you to stumble became less enticing and you began to walk in a new level of victory. You actually thought you might be free from that crippling menace. Then, after maybe even a lengthy period of time, you fell again. With it came the shame of hurting the Savior, the disappointment in yourself and the guilt that was all part of the fall. But this fall did not take our omniscient God by surprise and He will likely use it to strengthen you, slay a little more pride in your life and cause you to walk in a new level of humility. Paul's thorn in the flesh was left with him as long as he lived and it caused him to stay humble. This certainly does not lend approval to a sin, as it is abhorrent to God. But you repent and go forward in your faith seeking to honor and glorify your merciful Savior. Our freedom is not an ability to do what we want to do, but true believers are free from the condemnation of sin in Christ Jesus!

Might we be encouraged to listen carefully to our Father's guidance, hearing and then obeying? Now might we find this happening more and more as our conversation with our Father becomes more common and we know Him in increasing measure by studying His word? Does my new freedom mean I am now free to be bound to my new Master as a freed servant?

Gentle Shepherd, give us the grace to be obedient servants and avoid abusing our freedom.

Chapter Eight
Christian Life/Man's Responsibility

34. Believer's Freedom/Study Guide

What if God, the only all-powerful, all-knowing being...

1. knows His Son's death on the cross and resurrection back to life displayed His power and completely secured freedom and redemption, so that now anything is permissible for believers? **Hold on there!** Now we can do *anything*? What might that mean? Oh, there's more -- not everything is beneficial. (I Corinthians 6:12 & 10:23)

2. But what if I'm willing to take that risk? Well maybe, my old master is still in the hunt... (I Peter 5:8-9)

3. not for my soul but to destroy some part of me, or maybe me altogether, and he might make certain activities or old habits so alluring that I really want to get involved in them again. (Ephesians 6:12)

4. It certainly can be tempting because part of me received much pleasure from that old way of life, but in all honesty, those consequences always brought shame, pain, and just a big mess that needed cleaning up. Sometimes scars were left that are still with me. Maybe those scars are a good reminder when something sweet and tender says, "This is not a good idea..." (2 Timothy 1:14)

5. and as we resist the temptation... (James 4:7-8)

6. we are strangely empowered to turn away from the allurement. Might that sweet tender voice be the Holy Spirit that now indwells us, and if we find ourselves dwelling on and embracing the temptation, His voice becomes less and less noticeable? (I Thessalonians 5:19 & Ephesians 4:30)

7. Might we be encouraged to listen carefully to our Father's guidance, hearing and then obeying? Now might we find this happening more and more as our conversation with our Father becomes more common and we know Him in increasing measure by studying His Word? Does my new freedom mean I am now free to be bound to my new Master as a freed servant? (Romans 6:18 & Titus 1:1)

Gentle Shepherd, give us the grace to be obedient servants and to avoid abusing our freedom.

References for Believer's Freedom

1. I Corinthians 6:12

    I Corinthians 10:23

2. I Peter 5:8-9

3. Ephesians 6:12

4. 2 Timothy 1:14

5. James 4:7-8

6. I Thessalonians 5:19

    Ephesians 4:30

7. Romans 6:18

    Titus 1:1

Point of Truth: He whom the Son sets free is free indeed.

Practical Application: How might I walk in my freedom and honor the One who freed me?

35. Believer's Privilege

What if God, in helping us understand our position as servants to a loving Master that had purchased us from the slave market of sin would describe His servants in this light? After purchasing, and restoring ownership to its proper place, He informs us we are now free. In that freedom, by His Spirit, we realize that if we are truly His possession, we will willingly serve our new Master out of devotion and love, understanding the price that has been paid for our freedom. That price being the sacrifice of our Master's Son and the blood spilled to pay for the atonement of our sin; with sin always requiring the payment of blood, even from the beginning, when an animal was sacrificed to provide clothes to cover Adam and Eve's newly realized nakedness.

Consider that in our culture, those who are in positions of service are the ones who are not exactly the most respected as having done well. But Jesus reminds us the greatest is a servant to all, as He was. With that in mind, hopefully for even one in a most respected leadership position, we as believers will have the attitude of a humble servant. Then those of us that are truly in servant positions, as we work in our occupation, can rest in that position without any shame and serve those in authority over us in a way that brings them honor. Not always an easy thing to do.

Now, when we rightly obey His commands, as He instructs, we should in no way expect gratitude for doing our duty. As we find that in our obedience there is protection, we should be the ones that are grateful. As we mature, might we see that the world is involved in nothing that should cause us to desire it as we are simply passing through in a foreign land, journeying home? When we actually think this way, His commands are not burdensome as we overcome the allurements of the world. Might our response be after the day is done, and we have done all God has told us to do, "We are unworthy servants; we have only done our duty". With that, might we describe the duty as a privilege performed from a grateful heart in love? Might that also remind us as parents, it is our children's duty/

privilege to obey us, so might we resist the temptation to thank them for doing their duty and expect obedience?

Holy Father, grant us the grace and power to serve You in the way You direct us in Your Word.

Note: It is important to define the difference in a command and a request when considering this parable in Luke 17:8-10. For the sake of proper manners, we should say thank you when a request is honored but obedience is expected when given a command and a thank you should not be expected, whether from the Lord or as a parent.

35. Believer's Privilege/Study Guide

What if God, in helping us understand our position as servants to a loving Master who purchased us from the slave market of sin...

1. would describe His servants in this light? After purchasing and restoring ownership to its proper place, He informs us we are now free. (Romans 6:17-18)

2. In that freedom, by His Spirit, we realize that if we are truly His possession, we will willingly serve our new Master out of devotion and love, understanding the price that has been paid for our freedom, that price being the sacrifice of our Master's Son and the blood spilled to pay for the atonement of our sin... (I John 2:2)

3. with sin always requiring the payment of blood... (Leviticus 17:11)

4. even from the beginning, when an animal was sacrificed to provide clothes to cover Adam and Eve's newly realized nakedness. (Genesis 3:11 & 21)

5. Now, when we rightly obey His commands... (John 14:23)

6. as He instructs, we should in no way expect gratitude for doing our duty. (Luke 17:8-10)

7. As we find that in our obedience, there is protection, we should be the ones who are grateful. (I John 5:18)

8. As we mature, might we see that the world is involved in nothing that should cause us to desire it, as we are simply passing through in a foreign land, journeying home? (Hebrews 11:13)

9. When we actually think this way, His commands are not burdensome... (I John 5:3)

10. as we overcome the allurements of the world. Might our response be that after the day is done, and we have done all God has told us to do, that "We are unworthy servants; we have only done our duty"? (Luke 17:10)

11. With that, might we describe the duty as a privilege performed from a grateful heart in love? Might that also remind us as parents, it is our children's duty/privilege to obey us, so might we resist the temptation to thank them for doing their duty and instead expect obedience? (Ephesians 6:1-4)

Holy Father, grant us the grace and power to serve You in the way You direct us in Your Word.

References for Believer's Privilege

1. Romans 6:17-18

2. 1 John 2:2

3. Leviticus 17:11

4. Genesis 3:11

    Genesis 3:21

5. John 14:23

6. Luke 17:8-10

7. 1 John 5:18

8. Hebrews 11:13

9. 1 John 5:3

10. Luke 17:10

11. Ephesians 6:1-4

Point of Truth: A servant's duty is to serve his or her Master and obey His commands. We should serve out of love and devotion, not just duty. It is our privilege!

Practical Application: Does realizing that Jesus said it is our duty to serve Him, and that we are the ones who should be grateful, affect my walk as a believer and as a parent?

36. God's Bride

What if God, when He lovingly calls us His bride desires we look past the truth of the church being the bride of Christ and see the possibility of more? When He calls us His bride we are at first a bride in waiting. One word that is seldom used today for that position of a waiting bride is betrothed, meaning He has pledged His troth to us and also we have made the same pledge of our troth to Him. Ok, what in the world is troth? When we receive the Jewish Messiah, Jesus, as our Savior and Lord, it's the "Lord" part of "Savior and Lord" that troth affects. He says He is faithful and true and has pledged to return to consummate the marriage. He also says there will be a great ceremony, the Marriage Supper of the Lamb. But here we are waiting and serving our groom-to-be while living here as aliens doing His work. We are betrothed; we have pledged our loyalty, fidelity, and faithfulness to Him. Might these pledges be enabled by the power of the Holy Spirit to sanctify true believers, represented by the oil in the parable, reference #2? So when we flirt with the world, however that may apply, it is just that. The problem with flirting is we might go a little further and embrace the temptation and once we take that step, it is so easy to become part of the temptation in a relationship. Might that be fornication in a sense? At the very least, God will require us to obey His commands to truly be His bride, and she will be chaste.

Consider today, not only do marriages end daily in divorce, but a growing number of people are not even considering marriage. When these are the trends in the church, something is amiss. When the relationship involved in salvation is compared to that of a marriage it seems we are compelled to take this salvation relationship very seriously. It is obvious we are responsible to walk through the daily events of our lives with integrity, which are part of His commands for us. What about the last time you were tempted to compromise your position as a 'spoken for bride' and maybe even entered into that temptation. We know that cannot be the pattern or lifestyle of one that is truly born of God and may we be encouraged to seek righteousness as our lifestyle.

How's this for encouragement: He, in His loving manner, remembering we are but dust, knowing that we will fail, has given us an avenue to repentance and forgiveness. Might, as we grow in our understanding as His bride-to-be, avoid traveling the avenue of shame that is involved in repentance as we purpose, with He enabling us, to walk in obedience and anticipation of our soon coming groom!

Our Father, continually enable us to be Your faithful bride and deliver us from a wandering heart.

36. God's Bride/Study Guide

What if God, when He lovingly calls us His bride...

1. desires that we look past the truth of the church being the bride of Christ... (Ephesians 5:32)

2. and see the possibility of more? When He calls us His bride, we are at first a bride in waiting. (Matthew 25:1-13)

3. One word seldom used today for the position of a waiting bride is *betrothed*, meaning He has pledged His troth to us and we have made the same pledge of our troth to Him. Ok, what in the world is *troth*? When we receive the Jewish Messiah, Jesus, as our Savior and Lord, it's the "Lord" part of "Savior and Lord" that troth affects. He says He is faithful and true... (Revelation 19:11)

4. and has pledged to return to consummate the marriage. He also says there will be a great ceremony, the Marriage Supper of the Lamb. (Revelation 19:7-9)

5. But here we are, waiting and serving our groom-to-be while living here as aliens and doing His work. We are betrothed; we have pledged our loyalty, fidelity, and faithfulness to Him. Might the power of the Holy Spirit enable these pledges to sanctify true believers, represented by the oil in the parable, in reference #2? So when we flirt with the world, however that may apply, it is just that. The problem with flirting... (James 1:13-14)

6. is that we might go a little further and embrace the temptation... (James 1:15a)

7. and once we take that step, it is so easy to become part of the temptation in a relationship. (James 1:15b)

8. Might that be fornication in a sense? At the very least, God will require us to obey His commands to truly be His bride, and she will be chaste. (I John 3:4-6)

9. How's this for encouragement? He, in His loving manner, remembering we are but dust... (Psalm 103:14)

10. knowing that we will fail, has given us an avenue to repentance and forgiveness. (I John 1:9)

11. Might, as we grow in our understanding as His bride-to-be, avoid traveling the avenue of shame that is involved in repentance as we purpose, with Him enabling us... (Hebrews 2:18)

12. to walk in obedience and anticipation of our soon-coming groom! (Revelation 3:11 & 22:17)

Our Father, continually enable us to be Your faithful bride and deliver us from a wandering heart.

References for God's Bride

1. Ephesians 5:32

2. Matthew 25:1-13

3. Revelation 19:11

4. Revelation 19:7-9

5. James 1:13-14

6. James 1:15a

7. James 1:15b

8. I John 3:4-6

9. Psalm 103:14

10. I John 1:9

11. Hebrews 2:18

12. Revelation 3:11

    Revelation 22:17

Point of Truth: Jesus' bride will be chaste.

Practical Application: Have I been faithful to my coming groom, and if not, which areas am I tempted to flirt with the world?

37. True Believers

What if God kindly reminding us that if we are His children we will not forsake assembling together in worship and encouragement as a body? So is God encouraging us to go to church, or is this an essential command? Certainly being part of a church can be trying at times, just as anything else in which people are involved can be. Between different opinions and different doctrines, attending a church may seem daunting, especially if some of us were not raised in such an assembly. Do I have freewill and can choose by self determination to be saved, or has my salvation been completed and secured from before the foundation of the earth, and as He draws and enables, I receive Him as Savior because I was predestined to do so? Is salvation for all, or just the elect? How about women teaching men and just how much authority might a woman have in the church? So many things that divide, I wonder just who is the author of division? By contrast, Jesus himself said He came not to bring peace but to divide.

Consider when you drive in certain cities and towns it seems there is a church building on every block. Over the years one assembly splits from another and starts meeting in a separate location. Doctrine certainly is important and, as stated below, certain essentials are required, to be considered Christian. However, we really should not be surprised that Satan is constantly using individuals to be divisive in the churches. As we interact within the body and get to know one another there will certainly appear different interpretations of the Word that will tend to be divisive, but as God the Holy Spirit matures each one of His own, He is the one that can inspire and illumine His Word as we study some of these divisive subjects. Usually our opinion on a matter will not change anyone's mind as they have been led to certain conclusions from their own study. Now our opinions will influence others and many times there is a benefit in discussing matters not thoroughly defined in the Word. This also must be done in a loving and understanding manner as many brothers and sisters are strongly influenced by past traditions of parents, pastors and other influential people in their lives. You don't get too far telling someone they were taught incorrectly by those influential people, so let's purpose to honor each other, never compromise on the essentials and walk together in unity, to be about the important work of the kingdom and remember that God purposely inspired the Word, as He chose, to cause us to seek Him earnestly about some of these matters. It's kind of like Him to do things that way.

But God tells us to love one another. Funny how that changes everything. It's not an option, unless you're an unbeliever. As a matter of fact, He says we must love one another or we are not His. He also says that He is a God of order, and worship should be done in an orderly way. Might that leave some room for diversity with certain order in place while also gathering in spirit and in truth? So certain guidelines will be in place. We certainly won't be offering our children as sacrifices, or offering strange fire while attributing erroneous and heretical acts to the Holy Spirit. But in some ways, are we sacrificing our children when we want them to look, dress and act like the world in order to be accepted? But God again says that if you love the world, you are His enemy. He also spells out what's in store for His enemies. Might these thoughts cause us to realize if we are true believers, we will desire to gather with brothers and sisters, realizing the wheat and the tares are growing together? So there will be trying times, but it is assumed that we will meet together regularly with those whom we share the essentials of the faith, leaving the non essentials to our freedom in Messiah, with all else centered on and emanating from love that should be interwoven in everything!

Thank you, Almighty God, for the blessing of church assemblies.

37. True Believers/Study Guide

What if God kindly reminds us...

1. that if we are His children, we will not forsake assembling in worship and encouragement as a body? (Hebrews 10:25)

2. So is God encouraging us to go to church, or is this an essential command? Certainly being part of a church can be trying at times, just as anything else in which people are involved can be. Between different opinions and different doctrines, attending a church may seem daunting, especially if some of us were not raised in such an assembly. Do I have free will and can choose by self-determination... (John 7:16-17)

3. to be saved, or has my salvation been completed and secured from before the foundation... (2 Timothy 1:9)

4. of the earth, and as He draws and enables... (John 6:44 & 6:65)

5. I receive Him as Savior because I was predestined to do so? (Ephesians 1:4-5 & 11)

6. Is salvation for all, or just the elect? Can women teach men, and just how much authority might a woman have in the church? (I Timothy 2:11-15)

7. So many things that divide, I wonder just who is the author of division? (Titus 3:8-11 & Proverbs 6:16-19)

8. By contrast, Jesus Himself said He came not to bring peace but to divide. (Luke 12:49-53)

9. But God tells us to love one another. Funny how that changes everything. It's not an option, unless you're an unbeliever. As a

matter of fact, He says we must love one another or we are not His. (I John 4:19-21)

10. He also says He is a God of order, and worship should be done in an orderly way. (I Corinthians 14:26-39)

11. Might that leave some room for diversity with certain order in place while also gathering in spirit and in truth? (John 4:24)

12. So certain guidelines will be in place. We certainly won't be offering our children as sacrifices, or offering strange fire while attributing erroneous and heretical acts to the Holy Spirit. But in some ways, aren't we sacrificing our children when we want them to look, dress, and act like the world in order to be accepted? But God again says that if you love the world, you are His enemy. He also spells out what's in store for His enemies. (James 4:4 & Hebrews 10:26-27)

13. Might these thoughts cause us to realize that if we are true believers, we will desire to gather with brothers and sisters, realizing the wheat and the tares are growing... (Matthew 13:36-43)

14. together? So there will be trying times, but it is assumed that we will meet together regularly with those whom we share the essentials of the faith, leaving the nonessentials to our freedom in the Messiah, with all else centered on and emanating from love that should be interwoven in everything! (See: The Apostles Creed/The Nicene Creed)

Thank you, Almighty God, for the blessing of church assemblies.

References for True Believers

1. Hebrews 10:25

2. John 7:16-17

3. 2 Timothy 1:9

4. John 6:44

    John 6:65

5. Ephesians 1:4-5

    Ephesians 1:11

6. 1 Timothy 2:11-15

7. Titus 3:8-11

    Proverbs 6:16-19

8. Luke 12:49-53

9. 1 John 4:19-21

10. 1 Corinthians 14:26-39

11. John 4:24

12. James 4:4

    Hebrews 10:26-27

13. Matthew 13:36-43

14. The Apostles Creed/The Nicene Creed

Point of Truth: True believers will desire to fellowship and assemble with other believers to worship, to be encouraged, and to be challenged.

Practical Application: Do I regularly support and am I involved with the fellowship God has called me to, and how?

38. Love the Lord

What if God in His all-knowing wisdom would tell us that everything done prior to Jesus appearing on the scene, all the many pages that encompassed the Law and every truth the prior prophets had spoken could be summed up in two sentences? Love the Lord your God with all your heart and with all your soul and with all your mind and with all your strength. And the second is like it, Love your neighbor as yourself. With such a simple command, we may begin to understand why Jesus said the kingdom of heaven belongs to those who are like little children. A child is easily led, is very trusting, and is unaware that he or she is needy. With some proper encouragement, a child will do most anything commanded to do.

Consider the many times you have stated that you loved the Lord, not to mention how many in our culture would claim to believe in or know and love God. There does seem to be a disconnect in the statement and the reality. Remember that God said the beginning of knowledge and wisdom is the fear of God. Imagine yourself in the presence of the Perfect, Holy, Creator God, then consider how lightly we may use His name or easily we brush off His commands. I don't think that is the fearful, reverent awe of which He speaks. If we are truly His children and He has regenerated our hearts and made us alive spiritually; He says He will transform us to His likeness and in doing so we will start to realize what loving the Lord really is.

Might we mature to become as children. Wow, that's like many other unusual truths of the Word of God such as; give to receive, the last will be first, we must die to live, we must be bound to be free, be humble to come boldly, don't work so you can work, lose your life to save it, when I am weak, then I am strong and nothing in you that has not died will ever be raised from the dead. So would loving God completely, certainly mean obeying, serving, and worshipping Him alone? No idols and not using His name without a purpose, as He is God? So would that mean using God's name in a text or Facebook post without a purpose, equal using His name in vain? Well how about euphemisms that over the years have been adopted in casual conversation that sound like Jesus or God's name but are slightly different also be using His name in vain or without a purpose? Sounds like we may need to let our yes be yes and our no be no. And what about my neighbor? Does that mean if I love my neighbor, I will not lie to or slander him or her? I would not steal from my neighbor or have an immoral relationship with his or her spouse. It seems that something so simple can become so involved as we ponder the depths of God's wisdom. Maybe it would just be easier to stay a child, but I think I remember Paul and the writer of Hebrews getting a little upset about believers that continued to feed on milk.

Abba Father, will You give us the grace to grow as You empower and enable us.

38. Love the Lord/Study Guide

What if God, in His all-knowing wisdom...

1. would tell us that everything done prior to Jesus appearing on the scene -- all those pages that encompassed the Law and every truth the prior prophets had spoken -- could be summed up in two sentences? (Mark 12:29-31 & Matthew 22:37-40)

2. Love the Lord your God with all your heart and with all your soul and with all your mind and with all your strength. And the second is like it, Love your neighbor as yourself. With such a simple command, we may begin to understand why Jesus said the kingdom of heaven belongs to those who are like little children. (Matthew 19:13-14)

3. A child is easily led, is very trusting, and is unaware that he or she is needy. With some proper encouragement, a child will do most anything he or she is commanded to do. Might we mature to become as children? Wow, that's like many other unusual truths of the Word of God such as give to receive... (Malachi 3:10)

4. the last will be first... (Matthew 19:30)

5. we must die to live... (Galatians 2:19-20)

6. we must be bound to be free... (Romans 6:18-22)

7. be humble to come boldly... (Psalm 147:6 & Hebrews 4:16)

8. don't work so you can work... (Ephesians 2:8-9 & James 2:14-17)

9. lose your life to save it... (Luke 17:33)

10. when I am weak, then I am strong... (2 Corinthians 12:10)

11. and nothing in you that has not died will ever be raised from the dead. (C.S. Lewis, *Mere Christianity*)

12. So would loving God completely certainly mean obeying, serving, and worshipping Him alone? No idols, and not using His name without a purpose, as He is God. (Exodus 20:7)

13. So would that mean using God's name in a text or Facebook post without a purpose, equal using His name in vain? Well how about euphemisms that over the years have been adopted in casual conversation that sound like Jesus or God's name but are slightly different also be using His name in vain or without a purpose? Sounds like we may need to let our yes be yes and our no be no. (Matthew 5:37)

14. And what about my neighbor? Does that mean if I love my neighbor, I will not lie to or slander him or her? I would not steal from my neighbor or have an immoral relationship with his or her spouse. It seems that something so simple can become so involved as we ponder the depths of God's wisdom. Maybe it would just be easier to stay a child, but I think I remember Paul and the writer of Hebrews getting a little upset about believers who continued to feed on milk. (1 Corinthians 3:1-3 & Hebrews 5:12-14)

Abba Father, will You give us the grace to grow as You empower and enable us?

References for Love the Lord

1. Mark 12:29-31

   Matthew 22:37-40

2. Matthew 19:13-14

3. Malachi 3:10

4. Matthew 19:30

5. Galatians 2:19-20

6. Romans 6:18-22

7. Psalm 147:6

   Hebrews 4:16

8. Ephesians 2:8-9

   James 2:14-17

9. Luke 17:33

10. 2 Corinthians 12:10

11. C.S. Lewis, *Mere Christianity*

12. Exodus 20:7

13. Matthew 5:37

14. 1 Corinthians 3:1-3

    Hebrews 5:12-14

Point of Truth: Loving the Lord as He commands will reach into every area of our lives.

Practical Application: How might I love God and my neighbor genuinely and from a pure heart?

CHAPTER NINE
Christian Life / God's Sovereignty

39. Righteousness

What if God knowing the effect of the fall on all men the wicked and the righteous...

Wait a minute! What about God saying there are none righteous? Might that mean there are two types of righteousness, God's and man's? Maybe when He spoke about all man's righteousness being filthy rags He was comparing that to His perfect, holy righteousness? So what does He mean when He speaks of a righteous man? Might that be a man who would do what is right in man's eyes, he pays his bills, is upright and honest in all his dealings and his relationships, faithful to his wife and is honorable? Yet God describes that righteous man as "filthy" in His sight. With that in mind, we, too, might see the effect the fall has had on all men. We find ourselves desperately lacking and needing salvation; so hopefully, we start to understand why salvation is not of works but all about God and his mercy.

Consider the times you've beaten yourself up, knowing you failed miserably to keep up your end of being a believer in Jesus. But this is where God in His sovereignty makes all the difference in our relationship to Him. He foreknew, predestined, called, justified and gloried all that He has chosen to be born sons of God. He is not surprised by all the events in our lives, good and bad, and is using those as He transforms us into usable vessels for His purposes. Yes, even and especially the weak areas where we tend to fail Him the most. We are sealed by the Holy Spirit of God and born again into His spiritual kingdom. And He knows the hearts of the redeemed and will remove the excess flesh that tends to cause us to fail.

Might that also mean that there are two types of hearts in men, wicked and righteous? God in His omniscience would know that some righteous as well as some wicked will turn to Him, though the latter being less likely than the former. But some righteous would also turn away from Him and the wicked will continue in their wickedness. With that in mind reflect on this: at the very instant Jesus died on the cross, the very hand of God tore the veil that separated the Holy of Holies in the temple of the Jews from top to bottom. The separation was no longer necessary, as Jesus made the final perfect blood sacrifice, completely atoning for the sins of all men. With that atoning sacrifice Jesus' righteousness is now imputed to God's adopted sons and daughters as He saves and regenerates each one and we stand as righteous before Him. Before all this took place, is it possible that God, knowing the hearts of all men, predestined those that could be justly salvaged from the fall, and draws and enables them to turn to Him and He alone saves those who could justly be saved? Praise be to the Sovereign Creator God whose ways are beyond our understanding and desires all to be saved.

All powerful God, we bless and thank You for Your holy power and abundant mercy.

Chapter Nine
Christian Life/God's Sovereignty

39. Righteousness/Study Guide

What if God, knowing the effect of the fall on all men -- the wicked and the righteous...

1. *Wait a minute!* What about God saying there is none righteous? (Psalm 14:1)

2. Might that mean there are two types of righteousness, God's and man's? Maybe when He spoke about all man's righteousness being filthy rags... (Isaiah 64:6)

3. He was comparing it to His perfect, holy righteousness. So what does He mean when He speaks of a righteous man? Might that be a man who would do what is right in man's eyes -- paying the bills, as well as being upright and honest in all dealings and relationships, faithful to his wife, and honorable? Yet God describes that righteous man as "filthy" in His sight. With that in mind, we, too, might see the effect the fall has had on all men. We find ourselves desperately lacking and needing salvation, so hopefully we start to understand why salvation is not of works... (Ephesians 2:8-9)

4. but all about God and his mercy. (Romans 9:15-16)

5. Might that also mean there are two types of hearts in men, wicked and righteous? God, in His omniscience, knows that some righteous as well as some wicked will turn to Him, though the latter is less likely than the former. (I Peter 4:18)

6. But some righteous will also turn away from Him and the wicked will continue in their wickedness. (Ezekiel 18:5-22)

7. With that in mind reflect on this: at the very instant Jesus died on the cross, the very hand of God tore the veil that separated the Holy of Holies in the temple of the Jews from top to bottom. (Mark 15:38)

8. The separation was no longer necessary, as Jesus made the final perfect blood sacrifice, completely atoning for the sins of all men. (I John 2:2)

9. With that atoning sacrifice, Jesus' righteousness is now imputed to God's adopted sons and daughters, as He saves and regenerates each one and we stand as righteous before Him. (Romans 3:25-26)

10. Before all this took place, is it possible that God, knowing the hearts of all men, predestined those who could be justly salvaged from the fall, and draws and enables them to turn to Him... (John 6:44 & 6:65)

11. and He alone saves those who can justly be saved? Praise be to the Sovereign Creator God whose ways are beyond our understanding... (Job 36:26 & 37:5)

12. and desires all to be saved. (I Timothy 2:4)

All-powerful God, we bless and thank You for Your holy power and abundant mercy.

References for Righteousness

1. Psalm 14:1

2. Isaiah 64:6

3. Ephesians 2:8-9

4. Romans 9:15-16

5. 1 Peter 4:18

6. Ezekiel 18:5-22

7. Mark 15:38

8. 1 John 2:2

9. Romans 3:25-26

10. John 6:44

    John 6:65

11. Job 36:26

    Job 37:5

12. 1 Timothy 2:4

Point of Truth: Only God, is righteous and through Jesus (the image of the invisible God), imputes His righteousness unto those who are true believers.

Practical Application: How have I seen God work His righteousness in me, and do I cooperate with His work?

40. God's Field / Sanctification

What if God helping us understand our purpose as His servants would refer to us as His field? What might that mean from His point of view and ours? It might be since Paul is addressing the Corinthians as immature, he is reminding them, and us, that as with a piece of land, purchased for use, the owner is the one who decides what that use might be according to the type of land purchased. As with each of the elect, as we are purchased by our rightful owner, some pieces of land might have become dense forest, and to produce a useful product, must be clear cut. Well, that removes everything that is seen, but a field that is still full of roots and stumps can't be plowed. This is when the work really starts, as God patiently removes stumps and the connecting roots that go deep into the soil of our lives. It is hard work (from man's point of view) and very disturbing to the soil all around as roots of many kinds of depravity are ripped from the soil. With us, ripping out those roots may take a while, as we are not always cooperative. We want to cover up exposed areas and habits we really wanted hidden, and we might cling to them until we recognize that anything we cling to is really a god we are worshiping in an idolatrous relationship as we value that god more than the True Living God.

Consider the last time you were working in your garden or yard and how the plants or grass you desire seems to be the hardest to have success growing. Well part of the curse of the fall was on the earth, and thorns and thistles seem to dominate. That is, in a way, how it is in our lives with sin as it dominates the lives of unbelievers, and still has an effect in the lives of believers. You pull up that dandelion and its back in a short time. The only solution is to remove the complete root and that is exactly what God states He is going to do as far as sanctification is concerned in our lives. Where we try and fail, He knows the solution and is going to bring it about. And it's probably going to be painful. Oh well, no pain no gain. Hmm, that is so easy to say.

We might realize that at salvation we received a new heart, a heart of flesh. But might sanctification be the work that is taking place as that heart must be circumcised to remove the unnecessary flesh. Ouch! Well, we can be encouraged that the result will be a productive field bearing fruit for the Master, and He is the One that will do it.

Faithful Father, You are longsuffering and patient, loving and full of mercy, give us the grace to walk in obedience.

40. God's Field (Sanctification) /Study Guide

What if God, helping us understand our purpose as His servants...

1. would refer to us as His field? (I Corinthians 3:9)

2. What might that mean from His point of view and ours? It might be that since Paul is addressing the Corinthians as immature... (I Corinthians 3:1-2)

3. he is reminding them, and us, that as with a piece of land, purchased for use, the owner... (Ezekiel 18:4)

4. is the one who decides what that use might be according to the type of land purchased. As with each of the elect... (I Peter 1:1-2)

5. as we are purchased by our rightful owner... (I Corinthians 6:19-20)

6. some pieces of land might have become dense forest, and to produce a useful product, they must be clear cut. (Matthew 3:10)

7. Well, that removes everything that is seen, but a field that is still full of roots and stumps can't be plowed. (Matthew 15:13)

8. This is when the work really starts, as God patiently removes stumps and the connecting roots that go deep into the soil of our lives. It is hard work (from man's point of view) and very disturbing to the soil all around as roots of many kinds of depravity... (Matthew 15:19)

9. are ripped from the soil. With us, ripping out those roots may take a while, as we are not always cooperative. We want to cover up exposed areas and habits we really wanted hidden, and we might cling to them until we recognize that anything we cling to is really a god we are worshiping in an idolatrous... (Colossians 3:5)

10. relationship, as we value that god more than the True Living God. We might realize that at salvation we received a new heart, a heart of flesh. (Ezekiel 36:26)

11. But might sanctification be the work that is taking place as that heart is circumcised... (Romans 2:29)

12. to remove the unnecessary flesh? Ouch! Well, we can be encouraged that the result will be a productive field bearing fruit for the Master, and He is the One who will do it. (I Thessalonians 5:23-24)

Faithful Father, you are longsuffering and patient, loving and full of mercy; give us the grace to walk in obedience.

References for God's Field/Sanctification

1. I Corinthians 3:9

2. I Corinthians 3:1-2

3. Ezekiel 18:4

4. I Peter 1:1-2

5. I Corinthians 6:19-20

6. Matthew 3:10

7. Matthew 15:13

8. Matthew 15:19

9. Colossians 3:5

10. Ezekiel 36:26

11. Romans 2:29

12. I Thessalonians 5:23-24

Point of Truth: We will be sanctified if we are true believers; God will see to it.

Practical Application: Which roots might I be clinging to or hiding?

41. Idolatry

What if God in the process of conforming us into His likeness, as He reveals weaknesses in our lives that may often lead to sin, would show that each time we return to that sin, we are choosing idolatry? Might we need to recognize that whatever the sinful activity might be, that is only the fruit of what is being fed by a root of a problem deep in our lives. We may even feel that God has short changed us somehow by not making us as attractive or intelligent as we would like to be, or by not giving us abilities we would like to have. We are then tempted to search for a cause of our disgruntlement in other people such as parents, wives, husbands, siblings or friends. Wow! Sounds like we may want to blame someone else. But perhaps God, being in control of everything, is working through our decisions and choices that He already knows about, and in doing so, is making us usable vessels for His kingdom in spite of our weaknesses and self-described faults. That may help us remember that we are a necessary part of the body.

Consider every negative thought you can remember ever having about yourself. Now, think of the truth that you are a unique creation of God and you have a special purpose in His kingdom. As in a body, the parts that are truly important are unseen, and until something goes wrong we seldom think about them. We spend much time on the areas that are seen such as hygiene and our appearance, and it is important as we are representing our Savior. But in reality most of us are unseen parts in the body of Christ and, as with the human body, are necessary for the body to function. God has designed us to serve in whatever that part may be and that is where we will find our fulfillment. Also, those parts of the body that are seen, such as pastors/preachers and teachers will be judged more severely as their voice will impact and influence those who hear. Mindful of such a responsibility, those individuals should be sure of their calling and cautiously enter those public offices. It is our nature to desire to be like someone that we admire, and even try to conform ourselves to a likeness of that individual in our dress and appearance if we are enamored by them. The problem arises when we admire that individual more than God himself. It is a subtle form of idolatry and avoiding such a path is necessary to worship God alone.

What an encouragement when He reveals the true source of our idolatry, and when we confess and repent of it, He begins to enable us to overcome what at one time was a great weakness in our lives. Chances are we will always be vulnerable in that area, but with His power and His revealed knowledge in us about the weakness, the allurement of whatever it may be that used to cause us to compromise, becomes less and less attractive, even disgusting!

Increase our knowledge and understanding merciful Father, that we may worship You alone.

41. Idolatry/Study Guide

What if God...

1. in the process of conforming us into His likeness... (Romans 8:29)

2. as He reveals weaknesses in our lives that may often lead to sin... (Romans 7:7-12)

3. would show us that each time we return to that sin; we are choosing idolatry? (Colossians 3:5)

4. Might we need to recognize that whatever the sinful activity might be, it is only the fruit of what is being fed by a root problem deep in our lives? (I Samuel 15:23)

5. We may even feel that God has shortchanged us somehow by not making us as attractive or as intelligent as we would like to be, or by not giving us abilities we would like to have. We are then tempted to search for the cause of our disgruntlement in other people, such as parents, wives, husbands, siblings, or friends. Wow! Sounds like we may want to blame someone else. But perhaps God, being in control of everything... (I Timothy 6:15)

6. is working through our decisions and choices that He already knows about, and in doing so, He is making us usable vessels for His kingdom in spite of our weaknesses and self-described faults. (Isaiah 64:8)

7. That may help us remember that we are a necessary part of the body. (I Corinthians 12:14-27)

8. What an encouragement when He reveals the true source of our idolatry, and when we confess and repent of it... (I John 1:9)

9. He begins to enable us to overcome what at one time was a great weakness in our lives. Chances are we will always be vulnerable in that area, but with His power and His revealed knowledge in us about the weakness, the allurement of whatever it may be that once caused us to compromise becomes less and less attractive and even disgusting! (Romans 8:37)

Increase our knowledge and understanding, merciful Father, that we may worship You alone.

References for Idolatry

1. Romans 8:29

2. Romans 7:7-12

3. Colossians 3:5

4. I Samuel 15:23

5. I Timothy 6:15

6. Isaiah 64:8

7. I Corinthians 12:14-27

8. I John 1:9

9. Romans 8:37

Point of Truth: God will not tolerate idolatry among His people.

Practical Application: Are there some possible idols in my life, and what might they be?

42. Is He Lord?

What if God knowing that there would be many who would call Him Lord, that in reality, He doesn't even know them? Might that mean calling Him Lord and Him truly being Lord are not the same thing? As we first begin our journey as that of a disciple of the Messiah, we may not be able to grasp all that He being Lord of our lives might involve. But while we are spiritual infants, some miraculous things may happen. When babies cry, for example, and are somehow fed from somewhere, cleansed and more or less kept from killing themselves for a span of time until they are able to start caring for themselves. As babes in Christ, our Abba Father, cares for us and starts us on the road to truly being His servant. Along that road, we may miraculously be suddenly delivered from substance such as alcohol or drugs, for example, but as we grow we are weaned from the milk God is feeding us and it becomes our responsibility to take the meat of the Word, and ingest it so that we might truly walk as His servants.

Consider the stark proclamation Jesus made when speaking of a tree and its fruit. He said that a bad tree bears bad fruit and a good tree bears good fruit and that the fruit they bear is what they had to do. The trees were either good or bad and that is how they were to be recognized. Of course He was speaking of false teachers or believers portraying themselves as true believers. Then Jesus went on to speak of these people calling Him Lord and even doing miraculous signs in His name. The truth is that these individuals are unregenerate; flesh men and are of their father, the Devil. The signs they do are false signs and wonders and are designed to deceive true believers and cause them to stumble. They also may deceive other unbelievers into a false security of supposed believers by being part of these satanic wonders. It is part of the unseen warfare between God and the devil and Jesus calls them workers of iniquity/evildoers, sends them to their doom and proclaims He never knew them. Calling Jesus Lord is what a believer is compelled to do and there is certain fruit that accompanies that statement. His sovereignty is above all and a truly regenerated/born again believer will bear a measure of good fruit; but we are responsible to learn of Him.

We might learn that the fear of the Lord is the beginning of knowledge and wisdom. That acknowledging Him in all our ways is the key to Him influencing our decisions. Those decisions being described as "paths" in His word are for us to make and if we are not careful to acknowledge Him, other influences such as the world, the flesh and the devil might be involved. As we go down the path of those decisions, He reminds us that He is the One directing our steps, if we are His. Now as we ponder these things, we again might notice a balance of His sovereignty and our responsibility. Then there comes the stark reminder that understanding these things ends, as He says ultimately His sovereignty will outweigh all else as He directs our steps. Might the one that called Him lord, but is not known by Him, truly not have the heart of a humble servant willing to be directed as the Master wills and by His omniscience, He has always known that condition? What a reminder that He is the Master and we are His servants as He sees to it that His will is accomplished.

Sovereign Lord, as You work Your will and purposes in our lives give us the grace to see our dependence on You and the willingness to step up to our responsibility.

42. Is He Lord?/Study Guide

What if God...

1. knows many would call Him Lord, but in reality, He doesn't even know them? (Matthew 7:15-23)

2. Might that mean calling Him Lord and Him truly being Lord are not the same thing? As we first begin our journey as a disciple of the Messiah, we may not be able to grasp all that Him being Lord of our lives might involve. But while we are spiritual infants, some miraculous things may happen. When babies cry, for example, they are somehow fed from somewhere, cleansed, and more or less kept from killing themselves for a span of time until they are able to start caring for themselves. As babes in Christ, our Abba Father cares for us and starts us on the road to truly being His servant. Along that road, we may miraculously be suddenly delivered from alcohol or drugs, for example, but as we grow and we are weaned from the milk God is feeding us... (I Peter 2:2)

3. it is our responsibility to take the meat... (Hebrews 5:13-14)

4. of the Word, and ingest it, so we might truly walk as His servants. (Ephesians 4:13)

5. We might learn that the fear of the Lord is the beginning of knowledge and wisdom... (Proverbs 1:7 & 9:10)

6. that acknowledging Him in all our ways is the key to Him influencing our decisions. (Proverbs 3:6)

7. Those decisions described as "paths" in His Word are for us to make... (Proverbs 16:9a)

8. and if we are not careful to acknowledge Him, the world, the flesh, and the devil might be involved. (I Peter 5:8)

9. As we go down the path of those decisions, He reminds us that He is the One directing our steps... (Proverbs 16:9b)

10. if we are His. Now as we ponder these things, we again might notice a balance of His sovereignty and our responsibility. Then there comes the stark reminder that understanding these things ends, as He says ultimately His sovereignty will outweigh all else as He directs our steps. (Proverbs 20:24 & Jeremiah 10:23-24)

11. Might the one who called Him Lord, but is not known by Him, truly not have the heart of a humble servant willing to be directed as the Master wills, and by His omniscience, He has always known that condition? What a reminder that He is the Master and we are His servants as He sees to it that His will is accomplished. (Isaiah 46:9-10)

Sovereign Lord, as You work Your will and purposes in our lives, give us the grace to see our dependence on You and the willingness to step up to our responsibility.

References for Is He Lord?

1. Matthew 7:15-23

2. 1 Peter 2:2

3. Hebrews 5:13-14

4. Ephesians 4:13

5. Proverbs 1:7

    Proverbs 9:10

6. Proverbs 3:6

7. Proverbs 16:9a

8. 1 Peter 5:8

9. Proverbs 16:9b

10. Proverbs 20:24

    Jeremiah 10:23-24

11. Isaiah 46:9-10

Point of Truth: If Jesus is not Lord of everything in our lives, He is not truly our Lord.

Practical Application: Is there a possibility Jesus could say to me, "I never knew you, Away from me, you evildoers!" and how might I ensure that He knows me?

43. Holiness

What if God who loves us with a love beyond what we could ever accomplish or imagine would remind us that without holiness no one will see the Lord? Now as we embrace this truth and attempt to make holiness a part of our lives, there seems to be a slight difficulty. Every morning I awake and look in the mirror, I am reminded of how far I am from His holiness. The problem is we have to live with ourselves and only we and God really know the condition of our heart. But then might we recall, one, five or even ten years ago, and might we begin to see that He is truly faithful to His word, in that, even though we still have not attained His image, we are so much closer to it than we once were. Might we also be reminded that our holy Savior is at the Father's right hand making intercession for us and with such an advocate we can be confident that He will complete what He has started in us? I guess that would mean we are back to the sovereignty of God and responsibility of man balance, so knowing that He is going to do His part, that leaves just what up to me?

Consider just what true holiness is from God's point of view, and then we should realize the importance and the necessity of Jesus imputing His righteousness to our account. To think that I could ever be considered holy without Him is to think beyond reality. I'm not saying we should not strive to live a pure and upright life, however, if we really saw our true condition before God's holy standard it seems even though He is working sanctification in me daily by the power of His Holy Spirit I will always fall short. What I might consider a perfect heart toward Him is still tattered with clinging flesh, possibly in no more than challenging thoughts throughout the day. Those truths should cause us to look forward to the day when we are glorified in reality and can experience true holiness without the ball and chain of flesh. Jesus reminded us that beyond His Law, if we were able to keep that, there is more involved with our heart condition as he told us, if we lust after a woman or man in our heart, it is considered adultery. And further than that if we hate our brother that is considered murder. These thoughts may cause us to wonder if there is any hope for us, but our hope should be in Him, and that is where we must rest even as we mature and more real holiness becomes evident in our life.

What an encouragement to know that our Intercessor walked here in this foreign country, knowing every temptation that we may find alluring and will empower us to resist when we desire to do so! Father, grant us the grace to desire to resist temptation, and remind us that to receive the grace we so desperately need, we must purpose to walk in humility. And what about the empowering part? Do you really mean that by Your Holy Spirit, we have the same power within us that brought a dead man back to life? Wow! With that kind of power available, might we humbly seek holiness with a new vigor, knowing it is nothing in me, but what He is doing in me because my Advocate's blood completely atoned for my sin. May we be more and more like Him (Holy) each day because He is Holy!

Sovereign Lord, You are holy in all You do, and we honor and give You praise that You reckoned us as holy in Jesus Christ by Your power. Thank You for seeing to it that we are being made holy in real ways according to Your Word.

43. Holiness/Study Guide

What if God, who loves us with a love beyond what we could ever accomplish or imagine...

1. would remind us that without holiness no one will see the Lord? (Hebrews 12:14)

2. Now as we embrace this truth and attempt to make holiness a part of our lives, there seems to be a slight difficulty. Every morning when I awake and look in the mirror, I am reminded of how far I am from His holiness. The problem is we have to live with ourselves and only we and God really know the condition of our hearts. (Psalm 139:2-4)

3. But then might we recall one, five, or even ten years ago, and might we begin to see that He is truly faithful to His Word... (Psalm 33:4)

4. in that, even though we still have not attained His image... (Philippians 3:12)

5. we are so much closer to it than we once were? Might we also be reminded that our holy Savior is at the Father's right hand, making intercession for us... (Romans 8:34)

6. and with such an advocate we can be confident that He will complete what He has started in us? (Philippians 1:6)

7. I guess that would mean we are back to the sovereignty of God and responsibility of man balance, so knowing that He is going to do His part... (I Thessalonians 5:23-24)

8. that leaves just what up to me? What an encouragement to know that our Intercessor walked here in this foreign country, knowing every temptation that we may find alluring... (Hebrews 2:18)

9. and will empower us to resist those temptations when we desire to do so! (I Corinthians 10:13)

10. Father, grant us the grace to desire to resist temptation, and remind us that to receive the grace we so desperately need, we must purpose to walk in humility. (James 4:6)

11. And what about the empowering part? Do you really mean that by your Holy Spirit, we have the same power within us that brought a dead man back to life? (I Corinthians 6:14 & Romans 8:11)

12. Wow! With that kind of power available, might we humbly seek holiness with a new vigor, knowing it is nothing in me, but what He is doing in me... (Galatians 2:20)

13. because my Advocate's blood completely atoned for my sin. (I John 2:2)

14. May we be more and more like Him (holy) each day because He is holy! (I Peter 1:15-16)

Sovereign Lord, You are holy in all You do, and we honor and give You praise that You reckoned us as holy in Jesus Christ by Your power. Thank you for seeing to it that we are being made holy in real ways according to Your Word.

References for Holiness

1. Hebrews 12:14

2. Psalm 139:2-4

3. Psalm 33:4

4. Philippians 3:12

5. Romans 8:34

6. Philippians 1:6

7. I Thessalonians 5:23-24

8. Hebrews 2:18

9. I Corinthians 10:13

10. James 4:6

11. I Corinthians 6:14

    Romans 8:11

12. Galatians 2:20

13. I John 2:2

14. I Peter 1:15-16

Point of Truth: We, as God's children, must seek holiness.

Practical Application: Which parts of my life lack a touch of God's holiness, and how might I seek His holiness in those areas?

CHAPTER TEN
FAMILY

44. God's Protocol

What if God knowing the natural tendencies of His human creation, commanded a protocol that would cause both men and women to be stretched in an effort to obey those commands? That may bring to mind the Jewish judge in the time before God appointed a king over His people. During the time of the judges everyone did as <u>they</u> saw fit. With such a culture of disobedience to God's law we might find a resemblance to our own culture. Oh yeah, back to the Jewish judge who ordered a man. *Wait right there*! That judge was a woman, in authority over men? Might she be appointed by God, against His protocol as a judgment due to the culture of wickedness? Could be. And the man seemed hesitant to obey without her accompanying him. After a word or two concerning his hesitance to walk in his role as a man, together they went forward and defeated the enemy by God's hand and brought peace to the nation for forty years.

Consider, first of all, that God does actually have reasons and purposes as to why He has put this "protocol" in His word as a pattern for marriage. Also, consider that marriage is the institution He uses to describe Jesus' relationship with us and it is the first institution He established in Genesis. With Jesus, it is a spiritual application and the matter we are discussing is the nuts and bolts of real life. But the similarities concerning Jesus and His bride and our marriages are as follows; both reflect permanency, love and devotion to one person and those similarities are inseparable. The fact is, there is hard work involved in any marriage and a determination to honor one another should be central to a marriage that honors God. Divorce is not even in the vocabulary. As God has set an order, and in that order, there is a protocol for authority. As men and women are to submit to Jesus' authority humbly, women are to submit to their husband's authority. With that in mind, Jesus is always right in His actions and words and never mistreats His bride, the church. So husbands must lovingly lead their families carefully listening to his wife, while realizing her value to him as well as to the Lord and honoring that value always. Wives too, must respect their husband's God-given role and support his authority over the family as well as her specifically. She can support his leadership and humbly help her husband in areas of life where he may be weaker than she is. These areas may be many but submission still equals obedience to avoid God's disciplining judgment as with the time of the judges in Israel and specifically with Deborah and Barak.

Does that scenario resemble our culture today when men fail to step up to their appointed role as leaders and women willingly step into that role? Is it possible God equipped some women for leadership because of the demands placed on them as mothers and wives? But the protocol? When men do step up, love and lead and women willingly submit and respect, both being stretched to do so, and together they obediently walk in their God- given roles, might there be order and blessing due to obedience? What an encouragement to be obedient in our relationship with our spouses and to raise our children to obey God's word, especially when it stretches us.

You, loving Father, are a God of order and peace. Enable us to submit to Your Word; to honor You and those we touch every day.

Chapter Ten
Family

44. God's Protocol/Study Guide

What if God...

1. knowing the natural tendencies of His human creation, commanded a protocol... (Ephesians 5:22-27)

2. that would cause both men and women to be stretched in an effort to obey those commands? That may bring to mind the Jewish judge before God appointed a king over His people. During the time of the judges, everyone did as <u>they</u> saw fit. (Judges 17:6 & 21:25)

3. With such a culture of disobedience to God's law, we might find a resemblance to our own culture? Oh yeah, back to the Jewish judge who ordered a man. Wait right there! That judge was a woman, in authority over men? Might she be appointed by God, against His protocol, as a judgment due to the culture of wickedness? (Isaiah 3:12)

4. Could be. And the man seemed hesitant to obey without her accompanying him. After a word or two concerning his hesitance to walk in his role as a man, together they went forward and defeated the enemy by God's hand and brought peace to the nation for forty years. (Judges 4 & 5)

5. Does that scenario resemble our culture today when men fail to step up to their appointed roles as leaders... (1 Timothy 2:12)

6. and women willingly step into those roles? Is it possible God better equipped some women for leadership because of the demands placed on them as mothers and wives? But the protocol? When

men do step up, love, and lead, and women willingly submit and respect... (Ephesians 5:21)

7. both being stretched to do so, and together they obediently walk in their God-given roles, might there be order and blessing because of that obedience? What an encouragement to be obedient in our relationships with our spouses and to raise our children to obey God's Word, especially when it stretches us. (I Samuel 15:22-23)

You, loving Father, are a God of order and peace. Enable us to submit to Your Word to honor You and those we touch every day.

References for God's Protocol

1. Ephesians 5:22-27

2. Judges 17:6

    Judges 21:25

3. Isaiah 3:12

4. Judges 4 & 5

5. 1 Timothy 2:12

6. Ephesians 5:21

7. 1 Samuel 15:22-23

Point of Truth: God has established His order of authority regardless of changing opinions and cultures.

Practical Application: Have I struggled to accept God's order of authority, and how can I honor God by submitting to His protocol?

45. Husbands and Wives

What if God in His omniscience would tell us in love to stay with the wife of our youth knowing, sadly, that the divorce rate for His church would be no better than it is in the world? Might He also imply for a woman to stay with the husband of her youth since now she can also divorce her husband? In a time where the culture is in chaos and men tend to wilt away and woman tend to dominate; parents obey their children and God's Word is not taken as the final authority concerning morality or anything else! We should not be surprised that the world disregards and hates God, but when the lifestyle of His people displays no real difference than that of the world, might we benefit from a closer look to see what else He says?

Consider a man who has a loving and beautiful wife because that beauty comes from within and he should be content in every way. How easy it is to become bored with what we have and start being discontented. Even with a most beautiful wife one can easily be tempted to think wrongly of others and if desire is allowed to run rampant it always leads to sin. Desire is where sin always begins and this area is especially volatile for men and women. A woman seems to be able to sense a husband's wandering heart and many times she will do the same out of revenge. This downward spiral leads to untold sorrow and hurt and is what our enemy (Satan) is all about, destruction. We as believers must stop wrong desire as soon as it raises it head and then contemplate what might be prompting us in that direction. Then honestly discuss with our spouses and work to resolve whatever that difficulty may be. It is so easy when this is mentioned for the offended spouse to react incorrectly, but in love, talk these things through and possibly seek Christian counseling and realize quickly, desire acted on can destroy what God has joined.

When a man's eye starts to wander, and he acts on it, he doesn't realize the price involved as he sins against God and also his own well being. The reality may come to mind that the woman involved has the ability to say no, but is willingly and sometime aggressively, playing a part in there being a relationship. God's command for one wife is emphasized, except in the case of marital unfaithfulness. Some would say divorce was only allowed when that unfaithfulness, as Mary, Jesus' mother was falsely accused of, occurred during betrothal. Joseph was contemplating divorce when God assured him Mary had not been unfaithful. Does it seem that Jesus recognized a man's first wife is still one with her first husband, even after the world grants divorce in that anyone who marries her commits adultery and the one who divorced her causes her to be an adulteress. If we as men gaze at another woman's beauty, what a serious consequence to hear Jesus say if we lust after her in our hearts, from His point of view, we have already committed adultery with her. Some would say that when a man remarries after divorce he no longer is qualified for church leadership, as from God's point of view he has two wives. Might we also see that when our prayers are hindered due to our mistreatment of the weaker partner it is because God does not hear the prayer of one who has, or even regards, sin in his heart?

Father, grant us the grace of contentment that we might love our wives as You loved Your church and gave Your life for her.

45. Husbands and Wives/Study Guide

What if God, in His omniscience...

1. would tell us in love to stay with the wives of our youth... (Proverbs 5:18-19)

2. knowing, sadly, that the divorce rate for His church would be no better than it is in the world? Might He also imply that a woman stay with the husband of her youth since now she can also divorce her husband? In a time where the culture is in chaos and men tend to wilt away and women tend to dominate, parents tend to obey their children, and God's Word is not taken as the final authority concerning morality or anything else, we should not be surprised that the world disregards and hates God... (John 15:18-19)

3. but when the lifestyle of His people displays no real difference than that of the world, might we benefit from a closer look to see what else He says? When a man's eye starts to wander... (Proverbs 6:25-26)

4. and he acts on it, he doesn't realize the price involved as he sins against God and his own well being. The reality may come to mind that the woman involved has the ability to say no, but is willingly, and sometimes aggressively, playing a part in there being a relationship. (Proverbs 5:3-14)

5. God's command for one wife is emphasized, except in the case of marital unfaithfulness. Some would say divorce was only allowed when that unfaithfulness, as Mary, Jesus' mother, was falsely accused of, occurred during betrothal. Joseph was contemplating divorce when God assured him Mary had not been unfaithful. (Matthew 1:18-21)

6. Does it seem that Jesus recognized a man's first wife is still one with her first husband, even after the world grants divorce in that anyone who marries her commits adultery and the one who divorces her causes her to be an adulteress? (Matthew 5:31-32)

7. If we as men gaze at another woman's beauty, what a serious consequence it is to hear Jesus say if we lust after her in our hearts, from His point of view, we have already committed adultery with her. (Matthew 5:27-30)

8. Some would say when a man remarries after a divorce, he is no longer qualified for church leadership, as from God's point of view he has two wives. (I Timothy 3:2 & 12)

9. Might we also see that when our prayers are hindered due to our mistreatment of the weaker partner... (I Peter 3:7)

10. it is because God does not hear the prayer of one who has, or even regards, sin in his heart? (Psalm 66:18 & Isaiah 59:2)

Father, grant us the grace of contentment that we might love our wives as You loved Your church and gave Your life for her.

References for Husbands and Wives

1. Proverbs 5:18-19

2. John 15:18-19

3. Proverbs 6:25-26

4. Proverbs 5:3-14

5. Matthew 1:18-21

6. Matthew 5:31-32

7. Matthew 5:27-30

8. I Timothy 3:2 &12

9. I Peter 3:7

10. Psalm 66:18

    Isaiah 59:2

Point of Truth: Marriage is a holy institution, ordained by God, and should be entered into for life.

Practical Application: How might I guard myself against desiring someone other than my spouse?

46. Families / Kingdom of Heaven

What if God showing His love for children, as well as families, instructed His disciples not only to let the children come to Him, but also used them as examples of those to whom the kingdom of heaven belongs? When considering the collateral damage children suffer from divorce, might we seek even more to honor our wives and love them as the Messiah loves the church and died for her? Might also wives respect their husbands and encourage them with scriptural submission? With the Holy Spirit needing to stretch us a bit so we can obey the two previous commands, and desiring to be obedient and honor our merciful Savior, might we make every effort to walk in Him concerning marriage and family as we are blessed with the reward of children? As we willingly submit to our Savior, may we seriously resist the influences of the enemy and instead embrace the influence of the Word and His indwelling Spirit? In doing so, might we keep our families from becoming dysfunctional, and instead provide order and stability in the home... **Wait a minute**! Is there any such thing as a functional family?

Even with the blessings of the indwelling Holy Spirit and our hearts being circumcised because of sanctification, the day-to-day requirements of life still take their toll. With that in mind might we drop the pressure of performing and depend on the One who instituted family to enable us to be obedient and transparent in our relationships with our spouses and children, walking in humility before God and others, realizing we will fail? Let us confess and repent with a heart of gratefulness to the One who knows we are just dust! Now the balance: let's not let the previously mentioned realities give us excuses to be undisciplined, and let's instead strive for orderliness in our homes. May our homes be a small taste of the Kingdom of Heaven on earth as we lovingly require our children to obey while we as parents resist the temptation to win their approval and be their friends instead of their parents? Let us realize the time for friendship will come when they are adults!

Consider that believers are already part of the Kingdom of Heaven once we are adopted into God's family. Picture your home in your mind, and also, the fact that the Holy Spirit is there in you and your spouse as believers. As we live our lives might we be mindful of His presence and purpose to create an environment in our homes that honors God.

Now, let's take a look at the really difficult principle, as we soberly ponder God's protocol of Christ being the head of the church and the husband being the head of the wife. Might that also be part of the reason the Word tells women not to be in authority over a man as a man could never be in authority over Christ? Wow! So might that also mean God said women being in authority in certain types of roles are part of His judgment on the wicked nations? **Hold on there**!!! Both men and women are always suppose to listen carefully to those we are in authority over and take heed when needed, as we purpose to be servant leaders! Don't get angry and shoot the carrier pigeon; he's just bringing the message. Might it be if you have gone this far in these devotions you truly have a heart for God, so apply 2 Timothy 2:7☺!

Lord, we recognize You are sovereign and have created men and women for specific purposes and roles and we need Your grace to swim upstream against culture and political correctness to honor You!

46. Families (Kingdom of Heaven)/Study Guide

What if God, showing His love for children, as well as families...

1. instructed His disciples not only to let the children come to Him, but also use them as examples of those to whom the kingdom of heaven belongs? (Matthew 19:13-14)

2. When considering the collateral damage children suffer from divorce, might husbands seek even more to honor their wives and love them as the Messiah loves the church and died for her? Might also wives respect their husbands and encourage them with scriptural submission? (Ephesians 5:22-23)

3. With the Holy Spirit needing to stretch us a bit so we can obey the two previous commands, and with our desiring to be obedient and honor our merciful Savior, might we make every effort to walk in Him concerning marriage and family as we are blessed with the reward of children? (Psalm 127:3-5)

4. As we willingly submit to our Savior, may we seriously resist the influences of the enemy... (James 4:7)

5. and instead embrace the influence of the Word and His indwelling Spirit? In doing so, might we keep our families from becoming dysfunctional, and instead provide order and stability in the home... *Wait a minute*! Is there any such thing as a functional family? Even with the blessings of the indwelling Holy Spirit and our hearts being circumcised because of sanctification, the day-to-day requirements of life still take their toll. With that in mind, might we drop the pressure of performing and depend on the One who instituted the family to enable us to be obedient and transparent in our relationships with our spouses and children, walking in humility before God and others, realizing we will fail? (Proverbs 24:16)

6. Let us confess and repent with a heart of gratefulness to the One who knows we are just dust! (Psalm 103:14)

7. Now the balance: let's not allow the previously mentioned realities to give us excuses to be undisciplined, and let's instead strive for orderliness in our homes. May our homes be a small taste of the Kingdom of Heaven on earth as we lovingly require our children to obey while we as parents resist the temptation to win their approval and be their friends instead of their parents. Let us realize the time for friendship will come when they are adults! Now, let's take a look at the really difficult principle, as we soberly ponder God's protocol of Christ being the head of the church and the husband being the head of the wife. (Ephesians 5:22-23)

8. Might that also be part of the reason the Word tells women not to be in authority over a man... (1 Timothy 2:12)

9. as a man could never be in authority over Christ? Wow! So might that also mean God said women being in authority in certain types of roles are part of His judgment on the wicked nations? (Isaiah 3:12)

10. *Hold on there*! Both men and women are always supposed to carefully listen to those we are in authority over and take heed when needed, as we purpose to be servant leaders! Don't get angry and shoot the carrier pigeon; he's just bringing the message. Might it be that if you have gotten this far in these devotions, you truly have a heart for God? (2 Timothy 2:7)

Lord, we recognize You are sovereign and have created men and women for specific purposes and roles, and we need Your grace to swim upstream against culture and political correctness to honor You!

References for Kingdom of Heaven/Families

1. Matthew 19:13-14
2. Ephesians 5:22-23
3. Psalm 127:3-5
4. James 4:7
5. Proverbs 24:16
6. Psalm 103:14
7. Ephesians 5:22-23
8. I Timothy 2:12
9. Isaiah 3:12
10. 2 Timothy 2:7

Point of Truth: God's church is His Kingdom on earth, and our homes should be a small taste of that Kingdom.

Practical Application: How can I honor my spouse and the Lord and improve my parenting by applying His Word to my life?

47. Prodigal

What if God knowing the pain that would be caused when one's child, adult or teen, would turn from God and walk in sin, some for a season and for some the rest of their lives...would offer consolation but not necessarily as we might think? Seems that since God instituted the family our enemy has sought to destroy that institution, as it is the means to the Sovereign's seeking of a godly offspring. Even when the Lord refused Cain's inadequate offering and he slew his brother in envy and anger, might we draw the conclusion that Cain had a wicked and unredeemable heart? He was responsible for his actions, even though sin ruled and controlled him and he would not overcome it. In no way does this knowledge make the pain of what was done any more bearable to the parents, as they lost both sons, one son to death, and one to an unrepentant heart. Joyfully, however, they were reunited with Abel in eternity. As this pattern continued with Jacob and Esau certainly their parents wept at the thought that one desired to kill the other, and even though God protected Jacob, Esau's wicked heart did not and could not repent in a manner that God would accept. Esau was still responsible for his wickedness even though controlled by his master, sin. But what about David, the adulterer and murderer, as he is described as a man after the heart of God, spoken about him before he committed his wicked sins? Is it possible that the evidence that David always repented in a way that was acceptable to God revealed that his heart was redeemable as he realized it was God's mercy that provided repentance and forgiveness, and that, only through a humble and contrite heart?

Consider also that not every prodigal even in Scripture returned. The familiar story in Luke 15 ends well, however, remembering David's son Absalom, the ending was tragic as he lost his life and apparently never repented. Jesus told us trouble would be part of our life, but the thought of losing a child or maybe an adult child in death is tragic. But there is another kind of loss that is sadly a part of today's world more often than we might realize. Families are torn apart by broken relationships where one in their family is deceived into estranging themselves from their family thinking they are right in doing so. This is painful, however, if all means of reconciliation are attempted and refused, one is left to rely on God's grace and mercy and Jesus reminds us that if we love that "prodigal" more that we love Him we are unworthy of Him. How might that play out? Seemingly Jesus is teaching us first, if we truly love Him we will obey His commands. Then if an incident or situation leads to a decision to compromise the Scriptures in order to save a relationship, it seems we may love that "prodigal" more than Jesus. This leaves a true believer only to turn in faith to Jesus and trust in and depend on Him completely.

How we rejoice when a prodigal exhibits a repentant heart and places himself at the mercy of the Father. But sadly, Cain, Esau and Absalom remind us that the road that leads to life is narrow and few there be that find it. So what might be the consolation for the parents that cannot know if their prodigal will ever return? We can know that God is just and full of mercy and if that son or daughter can repent, even though he or she committed heinous sin, there is a place in his or her heart that will truly turn to Him and repent. Might we also take comfort in the possibility that if that son or daughter does not repent; he or she could not because of a wicked heart that will not turn to God? Hopefully we will avoid blaming ourselves as parents, even though we all fail. Nonetheless, each individual is responsible for his or her own sin and just possibly, God is big enough, that in His foreknowledge and power has predestined all that could turn, repent and be saved!

Give us the grace Father, to trust You and rest in You as we wait for Your will to be accomplished in each one of our lives and in the lives of those we love. Might we be available as You use us as vessels of mercy?

47. Prodigal/Study Guide

What if God, knowing the pain that would be caused when a child, teen, or adult turns from God and walks in sin, some for a season and some for the rest of their lives...

1. would offer consolation but not necessarily as we might think? Seems that since God instituted the family, our enemy has sought to destroy that institution, as it is the Sovereign's means of seeking a Godly offspring. (Malachi 2:14-15)

2. Even when the Lord refused Cain's inadequate offering and he slew his brother in envy and anger, might we draw the conclusion that Cain had a wicked and unredeemable heart? (Genesis 4:1-12)

3. He was still responsible for his actions, however, even though sin ruled and controlled him and he would never overcome it. (Jude 11)

4. In no way does this knowledge make the pain of what he did any more bearable to Cain's parents, as they lost both sons, one to death, and one due to an unrepentant heart. Joyfully, however, they were reunited with Abel in eternity. As this pattern continued with Jacob and Esau... (Genesis 27:41)

5. certainly their parents wept at the thought that one desired to kill the other, and even though God protected Jacob... (Genesis 28:13-15)

6. Esau's wicked heart did not and could not repent in a manner that God would accept. (Obadiah 1:8-10)

7. Esau was still responsible for his wickedness even though He was controlled by his master, sin. (Romans 9:19-24)

8. But what about David, the adulterer and murderer, as he is described as a man after the heart of God before he committed his wicked sins? (I Samuel 13:14)

9. Is it possible that the evidence that David always repented in a way that was acceptable to God revealed his heart was redeemable, as he realized it was God's mercy that provided repentance and forgiveness, and even then only through a humble and contrite heart? (Psalm 51)

10. How we rejoice when a prodigal exhibits a repentant heart and places himself at the mercy of the Father. (Luke 15:21)

11. But sadly, Cain, Esau and Absalom remind us that the road that leads to life is narrow and few there be that find it. (Matthew 7:13-14)

12. So what might the consolation be for parents who cannot know if their prodigal will ever return? We can know that God is just and full of mercy and if that son or daughter can repent, even though he or she may have committed a heinous sin, there is a place deep in his or her heart that will truly turn to Him and repent. Might we also take comfort in the possibility that if that son or daughter does not repent, he or she could not do so because of a wicked heart that will not turn to God? (John 5:40)

13. Hopefully we will avoid blaming ourselves as parents, even though we all fail. Nonetheless, each individual is responsible for his or her own sin, and just possibly, God is big enough that in His foreknowledge and power, He has predestined all that could turn, repent, and be saved! (Ezekiel 18:4)

Give us the grace, Father, to trust You and rest in You as we wait for Your will to be accomplished in each one of our lives and in the lives of those we love. Might we be available for You to use us as Your vessels of mercy?

References for Prodigal

1. Malachi 2:14-15
2. Genesis 4:1-12
3. Jude 11
4. Genesis 27:41
5. Genesis 28:13-15
6. Obadiah 1:8-10
7. Romans 9:19-24
8. 1 Samuel 13:14
9. Psalm 51
10. Luke 15:21
11. Matthew 7:13-14
12. John 5:40
13. Ezekiel 18:4

Point of Truth: Our Abba Father will run to meet us when we turn to Him in repentance, but there are those who will not turn.

Practical Application: How has God the Father patiently waited for me to return to Him, and what was it that so captivated me?

CHAPTER ELEVEN
ANGELS AND HEAVEN

48. Angels

What if God knowing that whenever He sent one of His messengers to do His bidding... there might be a tendency for His creation to worship the messenger? Even as John was given the Revelation of Jesus Christ to be recorded as part of God's Word, he fell to worship at the feet of the angel sent to him even though he walked and talked with Jesus. The angel instructed John, however, "Don't do it! I am a fellow servant with you and with your brothers, the prophets, and of all who keep the words of this book; Worship God!" As angels are supernatural beings created by God to serve Him as He pleases, one would think that to have the privilege to see one of these beings would cause there to be certain awe. Apparently, however, angels can appear as normal humans and not be recognized. It is interesting that the angels who were hurled from heaven with Lucifer in their rebellion were not given an opportunity to be redeemed as humans have after our fall. The elect angels must be very different beings as they do not marry, and with that apparently do not procreate. That may be the reason some would say there are no female angels. We do know, however, that the angels worship God and serve in a role of protection for God's chosen people; however, there are those that would say they don't sing because singing is reserved for those who have experienced the redemption from our fallen and lost position. When Christ's birth was announced the angels said, "Glory to God in the Highest and on earth peace to all men." In Job and in Revelation they seem to shout! Whether they spoke or shouted, however, probably doesn't matter either way, and hopefully won't affect our Christmas celebration.

What if God?

Consider the many situations where strange events that appear supernatural are observed, such as a religious statue shedding tears of blood. The unseen world is as or more active than the world we are a part of and the conflicts there are real. The incident recorded in Scripture of an unnamed angel being delayed in getting a message to Daniel and was helped by Michael, a chief prince in the hierarchy of God's angels, is evidence of this. Satan's unseen world is organized and is working with a purpose to kill, steal and destroy all of God's creation that he is allowed to be involved in. Our only protection is the omnipotent power of God over His powerful foe and the elect angels are part of that ongoing effort. It seems that Satan would try to duplicate all that God does so we must be diligent in our effort to be discerning.

We do know angels long to look into the matter of redemption and engage in battle against their fallen adversaries, which also are our adversaries. Might we be mindful that Satan and his demons (fallen angels) are real and powerful if we, as God's people give them room to do their destructive work in our lives? With this knowledge might we be more sensitive to the things of the world, which God says make us His enemy, and resist the allurements our adversary might offer.

Thank you Almighty God, for Your amazing work of creation and grant us the ability to be more aware of the unseen world and the warfare that is going on around us.

Chapter Eleven
Angels and Heaven

48. Angels/Study Guide

What if God, knowing that whenever He sent one of His messengers to do His bidding...

1. there might be a tendency for His creation to worship the messenger? Even as John was given the Revelation of Jesus Christ to be recorded as part of God's Word, he fell to worship at the feet of the angel God sent him, even though John walked and talked with Jesus. The angel instructed John, however, "Don't do it! I am a fellow servant with you and with your brothers, the prophets, and all who keep the words of this book; worship God!" (Revelation 19:10, 22:8-9 NIV & Luke 24:5)

2. As angels are supernatural beings created by God to serve Him as He pleases, one would think that to have the privilege of seeing one of these beings would cause certain awe. Apparently, however, angels can appear as normal humans and not be recognized. (Hebrews 13:2)

3. It is interesting that the angels who were hurled from heaven, along with Lucifer, in their rebellion... (Revelation 12:7-9 & Luke 10:18)

4. were not given an opportunity to be redeemed as humans have after our fall. The elect angels must be very different beings, as they do not marry, and with that they apparently do not procreate. (Matthew 22:30)

5. That may be the reason some would say there are no female angels. We do know, however, that the angels worship God and serve as protectors for God's chosen people; (Hebrews 1:7 & 14; Psalm 34:7 & 91:11)

What if God?

6. however, there are those who would say they don't sing because singing is reserved for those who have experienced the redemption from our fallen and lost position. When Christ's birth was announced, the angels <u>said</u>, "Glory to God in the Highest and on earth peace to all men." In Job and in Revelation they seem to shout! Whether they spoke or shouted, however, probably doesn't matter either way, and hopefully won't affect our Christmas celebration. We do know angels long to look into the matter of redemption... (I Peter 1:10-12)

7. and engage in battle... (Jude 9 & Daniel 10:12-13)

8. against their fallen adversaries, which also are our adversaries. Might we be mindful that Satan and his demons (fallen angels) are real and powerful if we... (I Peter 5:8)

9. as God's people give them room to do their destructive work in our lives? (Ephesians 4:26-32)

10. With this knowledge, might we be more sensitive to the things of the world, which God says make us His enemy, and resist the allurements our adversary might offer. (James 4:4-10)

Thank you, Almighty God, for Your amazing work of creation, and grant us the ability to be more aware of the unseen world and the warfare that is going on around us.

References for Angels

1. Revelation 19:10

   Revelation 22:8-9 NIV

   Luke 24:5

2. Hebrews 13:2

3. Revelation 12:7-9

   Luke 10:18

4. Matthew 22:30

5. Hebrews 1:7

   Hebrews 1:14

   Psalm 34:7

   Psalm 91:11

6. I Peter 1:10-12

7. Jude 9

   Daniel 10:12-13

8. I Peter 5:8

9. Ephesians 4:26-32

10. James 4:4-10

Point of Truth: God's elect angels are actively involved in carrying out God's will to accomplish His purposes.

Practical Application: Have I ever been inclined to worship God's creation instead of worshipping the Creator alone?

49. Going Home

What if God in His wisdom, knowledge and eternality (omnipresent), knowing that death would be, as a rule, a dreaded subject and that many would avoid the topic altogether? Certainly those who approach the end of their days that do not know Jesus, the Messiah of Israel, as their Savior and Lord, at best face the frightening prospect of standing before The One True Living God at the Great White Throne judgment and defending themselves without Jesus as an Advocate. God has said His wrath will be poured out on all unbelievers. Might that thought alone compel us to share the gospel with all we have the opportunity to share with? We can do so confidently, knowing that His sheep will hear His voice and as He draws and enables through His grace, whether we are plowing, planting, watering or reaping. Salvation is His work and what a privilege we have to be part of His work! With salvation in mind, we might automatically think of eternal life, but to get there we must remain aliens in this foreign land. We certainly do not want to make light of the kingdom work we are doing while we are here, but let's consider going home.

Consider the place that is being occupied by all the believing sons and daughters of God, heaven. Although, only since Jesus was crucified and was resurrected has heaven been the dwelling place for the redeemed. Jesus referred to heaven as paradise. Hades (Sheol) was the dwelling place for all the dead, righteous and wicked, before the atonement. This was because death at that time still held all men captive; however, Jesus defeated death, the grave, and sin with His perfect sacrifice. Now completed, He victoriously invaded Hades (Sheol) and released the captive Old Testament saints, Jew and Gentile, and took them in his train as He ascended to paradise. Now consider this, paradise (heaven) is just a temporary home! When Jesus returns in what is referred to as the second coming (not the rapture) all His adopted sons and daughters (His spiritual Israel) will accompany Him, and as Satan, as well as the Antichrist, is defeated at the end of the Great Tribulation we will assist Jesus Christ in establishing His millennial kingdom on this earth. Then we will function in that kingdom for 1000 years in our glorified position as He brings all things back unto Himself.

What if God?

When we start to contemplate the fact that God says we cannot even imagine what is in store for us, might that alone prompt us to want to be there. I'm not even thinking of the new heaven and earth that will come down after the 1000-year reign of Messiah. I'm thinking of just being with Him, not to mention all those who have gone on before us with whom we will be reunited! Might we say, like Paul, for me to live is Christ, and to die is gain, knowing that to be absent from the body is to be present with the Lord? Hopefully these truths will help us not to be anxious as we think of death, as God says His servant's death is precious in His sight. We may even find ourselves holding onto the things of this world with an increasingly loose grip, as they become less and less important, and rejoice in knowing that God said when the righteous perish, there is a reason only those who study His Word will understand.

Prince of Peace, give us courage to be obedient here and to anticipate what You have prepared for us, Your children.

49. Going Home/Study Guide

What if God, in His wisdom, knowledge, and eternality (omnipresence)...

1. knew that death would be, as a rule, a dreaded subject and that many would avoid the topic altogether? Certainly those who approach the end of their days and do not know Jesus, the Messiah of Israel, as their Savior and Lord, at best they face the frightening prospect of standing before The One True Living God at the Great White Throne judgment... (Revelation 20:11-15)

2. and defending themselves without Jesus as their Advocate. (I John 2:1-2)

3. God has said His wrath will be poured out on all unbelievers. (John 3:36 & Romans 2:6-8)

4. Might that thought alone compel us to share the gospel with everyone we have the opportunity to share with? We can do so confidently, knowing that His sheep will hear His voice... (John 10:4-5 & 14-16)

5. and as He draws and enables... (John 6:44 & 6:65)

6. through His grace... (Ephesians 2:8-9)

7. whether we are plowing, planting, watering, or reaping. Salvation is His work... (Psalm 68:20)

8. and what a privilege we have to be part of His work! With salvation in mind, we might automatically think of eternal life, but to get there we must remain aliens in this foreign land. (Hebrews 11:13)

9. We certainly do not want to make light of the Kingdom work we are doing while we are here, but let's consider going home. When we

start to contemplate the fact that God says we cannot even imagine what is in store for us... (I Corinthians 2:9)

10. might that alone prompt us to want to be there? I'm not even thinking of the new heaven and earth that will come down... (Revelation 21:1-3)

11. after the thousand-year reign of the Messiah. I'm thinking of just being with Him, not to mention all those who have gone on before us who we will be reunited with! Might we say, like Paul, for me to live is Christ, and to die is gain... (Philippians 1:21)

12. knowing that to be absent from the body is to be present with the Lord? (2 Corinthians 5:6-8)

13. Hopefully these truths will help us not to be anxious as we think of death, as God says His servant's death is precious in His sight. (Psalm 116:15)

14. We may even find ourselves holding onto the things of the world with an increasingly loose grip, as they become less and less important, and rejoice in knowing that God said when the righteous perish, there is a reason only those who study His Word will understand. (Isaiah 57:1-2)

Prince of Peace, give us courage to be obedient here and to anticipate what You have prepared for us, Your children.

References for Going Home

1. Revelation 20:11-15

2. 1 John 2:1-2

3. John 3:36

    Romans 2:6-8

4. John 10:4-5

    John 10:14-16

5. John 6:44

    John 6:65

6. Ephesians 2:8-9

7. Psalm 68:20

8. Hebrews 11:13

9. 1 Corinthians 2:9

10. Revelation 21:1-3

11. Philippians 1:21

12. 2 Corinthians 5:6-8

13. Psalm 116:15

14. Isaiah 57:1-2

Point of Truth: Every soul will stand before God in judgment.

Practical Application: How might my thoughts concerning death honor God?

CHAPTER TWELVE
A Sovereign God

50. God's Ownership

What if God knowing just how desperate the lost soul is, predestined all those who could (would) believe at a time when His ownership of that soul had not been compromised, before the foundation of the world? When God declares all living souls are His but then declares we were purchased by the Lamb, it appears that ownership was compromised. Before the foundation of the world He was the legal owner of all souls, and in predestining at this time did it insure His will and purposes would be accomplished concerning the war that Satan had declared against Him? Also, when He declares all the earth is His and everything in it, that is ultimately true since He declares judgment and sentence on Satan, his demons and sadly all those who would (could) not turn to Him in repentance. It may seem that those mentioned are free to do as they choose but ultimately God has determined their destiny.

Consider that predestination is one of the most divisive doctrines found in the Word of God. However, no matter how hard it is tried there is no getting around this truth. God predestined the elect according to His will and pleasure. He chose us in Him! We will not go any further as to whether that means He saw what we would do or determined what we would do. But there is the possibility; predestination is a necessary action (strategy) in God's ongoing war with Satan. Scripture does not speak to this and we are simply considering the possibility, not teaching this strategy as doctrine. However, the loss of ownership is doctrine, as at the fall, all mankind became slaves to sin. Thus being subjected to a new owner, Satan, until God, in a violent act of war frees us from our captive position. But why doesn't He free everyone. Some would hold to freewill and say that a man refuses the offer of salvation, while others say man has no freewill and is not able to receive salvation, even when offered, without God first regenerating that man or woman.

When we consider that we are bought with a price, might that mean when man fell, we became slaves to a ruthless owner until we are saved? But God saves those whom He determines can (will) turn to Him, and when we are saved, He tells us we are not our own. Rather, we are now once again owned by the Sovereign One (God). With this in mind, as each of His are born, at just the appointed time, He draws and enables us to receive Him, by His grace, in order that we might realize that salvation is of God alone, by faith alone, through grace alone and for His glory alone. In doing such a marvelous work, He provided us with every good gift needed to accomplish His good works He had prepared in advance. This had nothing to do with us. It is all in God's sovereign counsel, done justly by Him. With such a profound truth in mind, we might be humbled and marvel at His love and majesty that all we can do when considering these things is shake our heads and fall face down in worship of such a great and merciful God. That same loving God desiring that all could (would) come to Him reminds us that He has the emotion of sorrow at the thought of the wicked perishing without Him and their doom.

Sovereign God, may we accept You as You have revealed Yourself in Your Word and resist the temptation to add to that Word.

Chapter Twelve
A Sovereign God

50. God's Ownership/Study Guide

What if God, knowing just how desperate the lost soul is...

1. predestined all those who could (would) believe... (Ephesians 1:4-5 & 11)

2. at a time when His ownership of that soul had not been compromised, before the foundation of the world? When God declares all living souls are His... (Ezekiel 18:4)

3. but then declares we were purchased by the Lamb... (Revelation 5:9)

4. it appears that ownership was compromised. Before the foundation of the world He was the legal owner of all souls, so did predestining at this time ensure His will and purposes would be accomplished concerning the war that Satan had declared against Him? Also, when He declares all the earth is His... (Psalm 24:1)

5. and everything in it, that is ultimately true since He declares judgment and sentence on Satan, his demons, and sadly all those who would (could) not turn to Him in repentance. It may seem that those mentioned are free to do as they choose, but ultimately God has determined their destiny. When we consider that we are bought with a price, might that mean when man fell, we became slaves to a ruthless owner until we are saved? (John 8:34)

6. But God saves those whom He determines can (will) turn to Him, and when we are saved, He tells us we are not our own. (I Corinthians 6:19-20)

7. Rather, we are now once again owned by the Sovereign One (God). With this in mind, as each of His are born, at just the appointed time... (Acts 13:48)

8. He draws and enables us to receive Him... (John 6:44 & 6:65)

9. by His grace, in order that we might realize salvation is of God alone, by faith alone, through grace alone, and for His glory alone. In doing such a marvelous work, He provided us with every good gift needed to accomplish His good works He had prepared in advance. (Ephesians 2:4-10)

10. This had nothing to do with us. It is all in God's sovereign counsel, done justly by Him. (Romans 9:14 & Job 40:8)

11. With such a profound truth in mind, we might be humbled and marvel at His love and majesty that all we can do when considering these things is shake our heads and fall face down in worship of such a great and merciful God. That same loving God desiring that all could (would) come to Him... (1 Timothy 2:4)

12. reminds us that He feels sorrow at the thought of the wicked perishing without Him and the doom they face. (Ezekiel 18:23 & 32)

Sovereign God, may we accept You as You have revealed Yourself in Your Word and resist the temptation to add to that Word.

References for God's Ownership

1. Ephesians 1:4-5

    Ephesians 1:11

2. Ezekiel 18:4

3. Revelation 5:9

4. Psalm 24:1

5. John 8:34

6. I Corinthians 6:19-20

7. Acts 13:48

8. John 6:44

    John 6:65

9. Ephesians 2:4-10

10. Romans 9:14

    Job 40:8

11. I Timothy 2:4

12. Ezekiel 18:23 & 32

Point of Truth: God is the creator and ultimate owner of all His creation.

Practical Application: How does Satan's role in compromising God's ownership affect my understanding of redemption?

51. God's Sovereign Choice

What if God knowing the hearts of all men He created, the wicked and the righteous, in His omniscience knew even the righteous would be scarcely saved? He molded the objects of His mercy, which He prepared in advance for glory, to show the riches of His glory. In contrast, showing His wrath and making His power known, He bore with great patience the objects of His wrath prepared for destruction. *Hold on a minute*! Don't get lost thinking God purposely created certain individuals to be destined for destruction, but just maybe God, truly being omniscient and taking responsibility for giving life to all souls, knew all those who would (could) not turn to Him (man's responsibility) for salvation and ultimately are created for destruction?

Consider, as we delve into controversial, deep waters, that it is difficult to say this trying part of Scripture is speaking only of nations or God's messengers. It seems as the heart of man is spoken of so often as to its wickedness before regeneration, that it is not a stretch to say it is at least part of what God sees when determining the destiny of His creation. Some men's hearts may be past a point in wickedness that God has appointed redeemable. We can know that everything God does is just and perfect. With that in mind, we can also know that no one will be in heaven or hell mistakenly. God does not reveal exactly what His measuring scale is other than His will and pleasure; but maybe that is done purposely by Him to cause us to think of Him properly and increase the necessity for us to trust Him as He reveals Himself in His Word. We can also know that the Holy Spirit goes where it desires, not where it is asked to go. If man is truly in captivity to Satan and in his flesh cannot please God, as scripture teaches, it does seem regeneration (being born again) is a necessary first act on God's part in redemption. After that, one can hear the Gospel and see the need to be saved.

Now God might need to stretch us just a bit to accept this, but we must remember He is just! And what if this has been part of His purpose from the first man and through every covenant dispensation? He has shown His patience at the event of every wicked act throughout history, as He patiently observed. Sometimes intervening but not as a rule as He, on His timetable, has revealed Himself to the nations, revealed Himself in the giving of His Law, and then ultimately the giving of Himself; that the objects of mercy, both Jew and Gentile might be joined in a mysterious union nourished by the same patient vine. Might this be part of how God is reserving for Himself a remnant from every generation and at the end of this age all those objects of mercy, His spiritual Israel, are and will be the ruling citizens of His kingdom?

Ah, Lord God, You have made the heavens and the earth by Your great power and outstretched arm. Nothing is too difficult for You.

51. God's Sovereign Choice/Study Guide

What if God...

1. knowing the hearts of all men He created... (Matthew 9:4)

2. the wicked and the righteous... in His omniscience knew even the righteous would be scarcely saved? (1 Peter 4:18)

3. He molded the objects of His mercy, which He prepared in advance for glory, to show the riches of that glory. In contrast, showing His wrath and making His power known, He bore with great patience the objects of His wrath prepared for destruction. (Romans 9:22-24)

4. *Hold on a minute!* Don't get lost thinking God purposely created certain individuals to be destined for destruction, but just maybe God, being truly omniscient and taking responsibility for giving life to all souls, knew all those who would (could) not turn to Him for salvation (which is man's responsibility) and ultimately are created for destruction? Now God might need to stretch us just a bit to accept this, but we must remember He is just! (Job 40:8-14 & Acts 17:30-32)

5. And what if this has been part of His purpose from the first man and through every covenant dispensation? He has shown His patience at the event of every wicked act throughout history... (Psalm 33:14)

6. as He patiently observed. (Romans 3:25)

7. Sometimes intervening but not as a rule, as He, on His timetable, has revealed Himself to the nations... (Psalm 98:2)

8. revealed Himself in the giving of His Law... (Psalm 147:19-20)

9. and then ultimately the giving of Himself... (John 10:11 & 3:16)

10. that the objects of mercy, both Jew and Gentile, might be joined in a mysterious union... (Ephesians 3:6 & Galatians 3:14)

11. nourished by the same patient vine. (Romans 11:17)

12. Might this be part of how God is reserving for Himself a remnant... (Romans 11:4-8)

13. from every generation, and at the end of this age all those objects of mercy, His spiritual Israel... (Romans 2:28-29 & Galatians 3:6-9)

14. are and will be the ruling citizens of His kingdom? (2 Timothy 2:11-12)

Ah, Lord God, You have made the heavens and the earth by Your great power and outstretched arm. Nothing is too difficult for You.

References for God's Sovereign Choice

1. Matthew 9:4

2. 1 Peter 4:18

3. Romans 9:22-24

4. Job 40:8-14

    Acts 17:30-32

5. Psalm 33:14

6. Romans 3:25

7. Psalm 98:2

8. Psalm 147:19-20

9. John 10:11

    John 3:16

10. Ephesians 3:6

    Galatians 3:14

11. Romans 11:17

12. Romans 11:4-8

13. Romans 2:28-29

    Galatians 3:6-9

14. 2 Timothy 2:11-12

Point of Truth: God is sovereign over all His creation and acts according to His will and purposes.

Practical Application: Does this teaching cause me to think of God in a different way? How?

52. All Israel Will Be Saved

What if God exercising His sovereign reign over mankind and nations would make a remarkable statement through His servant Paul that "All Israel will be saved"? Remarkable indeed when one is reminded of, if nothing else, that God proclaimed every wicked king of Israel and many of Judah's over all the years past, did evil in the eyes of the Lord. Much of this evil had to do with the fact that they offered their children as human sacrifices to the wicked idols Israel had worshipped over the years. This particular sin was a detestable act in the sight of God that He warned against over and over again, and in truth, these sacrifices were actually made to demons. Even the wise King Solomon was possibly caught up in this practice as he built alters, and his wives burnt offerings and sacrificed to their gods, however, since this man wrote some of God's Word might we cautiously assume he is considered saved? If that is the case, we will need to assume at some point he realized his evil, humbled himself and prayed, sought God's face and repented of his sin.

What does it mean to ask, "Will every Jew be saved?" Might it be that all from Israel are not Israel and one is a Jew only if he is one inwardly? When considering these thoughts might we remember Jesus' example of the rich man and Lazarus? When the rich man in the story died, he went to Hades (Sheol) and was in torment. Well this fellow was a prominent Jew and it appears he was not saved. Also, Jesus in speaking to the "The Jews" at one particular feast, bluntly told these men they did not believe because they were not His sheep. These also were prominent Jews, evidently lost. So is it possible, there is a deeper meaning to Paul's statement that all Israel will be saved?

Consider that there are at least three different interpretations of this text of scripture and I am presenting the one that seems to fit in the whole of God's message in the Word, in my opinion. God is a spirit and His kingdom is a spiritual kingdom made up of all tongues, tribes and nations. This does not in any way remove the nation of Israel's importance in the whole of scripture, nor does it remove the nation of Israel's role in God's millennial kingdom. Jesus is the Jewish messiah and fortunately it has been God's plan all along, to also redeem a certain number of Gentiles into the nourishing vine of that same Messiah. It also is reliable to conclude that there is evidence observed in the lifestyle; when God regenerates a captive of Satan and frees that individual. This was true in the Old as well as the New Testament so it seems only a few of all humanity are recreated into Christ as a spirit man. But that few will be many, even as the sand of the seashore, in number with all of recorded history considered.

Is it possible that over all the centuries from creation, Adam and Eve, Abel, and then beginning with the line of Seth that led to Noah, Job, and right on through God's covenant with Abraham, in establishing the nation of Israel, giving the Law through that nation and then the new covenant through Jesus Christ, that God in His sovereignty has always had a people, a remnant, that through His sovereign counsels, He enabled to turn to Him and believe in Him by granting the gift of faith and He counted them as righteous? Is it possible that His spiritual Israel is from every tribe and tongue through the centuries, with those different groups looking forward to their resurrected Savior before the atonement on the cross and since the atonement looking back to the cross and the resurrection? Wow, and is it just possible all these people, and the ones yet to be gathered, are the spiritual children of Abraham, all of whom will be saved by a loving merciful God, who in His omniscience, knows their hearts could (would) turn to Him? In no way does this give us an excuse not to witness and support missions, but hopefully will motivate us to be all the more anxious to compel them to come! And possibly after the "church age," a meaning more in context with the theme of Romans 11, is that when the Messiah returns to rule the earth with an iron scepter, the entire nation of Israel will then, in the thousand-year reign, accept its Messiah!

Oh the depth and the riches of the wisdom and knowledge of You, oh God! How unsearchable Your judgments and paths beyond tracing! Who has been Your counselor? Who has ever given to You God, that you should repay him? For from You and through You and to You are all things. To You be the glory forever! Amen.

52. All Israel Will Be Saved/Study Guide

What if God, exercising His sovereign reign over mankind and nations...

1. would make a remarkable statement through His servant Paul that "All Israel will be saved"? (Romans 11:26)

2. Remarkable indeed when one is reminded of, if nothing else, that God proclaimed every wicked king of Israel and many of Judah's over all the years past, did evil in the eyes of the Lord. (2 Kings 13:2; 14:24; & 15:9, 18, 24, & 28)

3. Much of this evil had to do with the fact that they offered their children as human sacrifices to the wicked idols Israel had worshipped over the years. This particular sin was a detestable act in the sight of God that He warned against over and over again, and in truth, these sacrifices were actually made to demons. (Psalm 106:34-43)

4. Even the wise King Solomon was possibly caught up in this practice as he built altars, and his wives burnt offerings and sacrificed to their gods... (1 Kings 11:7-8)

5. however, since this man wrote some of God's Word, might we cautiously assume he is considered saved? If that is the case, we will need to assume at some point he realized his evil, humbled himself, prayed, sought God's face, and repented of his sin. (2 Chronicles 7:14)

6. What does it mean to ask, "Will every Jew be saved?" Might it be that all from Israel are not Israel and one is a Jew only if he or she is one inwardly? (Romans 9:6 & 2:28-29)

7. When considering these thoughts, might we remember Jesus' example of the rich man and Lazarus? (Luke 16:19-31)

8. When the rich man in the story died, he went to Hades and was in torment. Well, this fellow was a prominent Jew and it appears he was not saved. Also, Jesus, in speaking to the "The Jews" at one particular feast, bluntly told these men they did not believe because they were not His sheep. (John 10:26)

9. These also were prominent Jews, evidently lost. So possibly, there is a deeper meaning to Paul's statement that all Israel will be saved. Is it possible that over all the centuries from:

    - Adam and Eve
    - to Abel
    - to the line of Seth
    - which led to Noah, Job, and God's covenant with Abraham to establish the nation of Israel, through whom He gave the Law
    - and finally to the new covenant through Jesus Christ
    - that God, in His sovereignty, has always had a people, a remnant... (Romans 11:4-5)

10. that through His sovereign counsels... (Job 38:2-5)

11. He enabled to turn to Him and believe in Him by granting the gift of faith, and He counted them righteous? (James 2:23)

12. Is it possible, that His spiritual Israel from every tribe and tongue... (Revelation 5:9)

13. through the centuries has looked forward to their resurrected Savior before the atonement on the cross and has looked back to the cross and the resurrection since the atonement? Wow! And is it just possible all these people, and the ones yet to be gathered, in are the spiritual children of Abraham... (Galatians 3:6-9 & 6:14-16)

14. all of whom will be saved by a loving merciful God, who in His omniscience, knows that their hearts could (would) turn to Him?

In no way does this give us an excuse not to witness and support missions, but hopefully it will motivate us to be all the more anxious to compel them to come! And possibly after the "church age," a meaning more in context with the theme of Romans 11, is that when the Messiah returns to rule the earth with an iron scepter, the entire nation of Israel will then, in the thousand-year reign, accept its Messiah! (Revelation 2:27, 12:5 & 19:15)

Oh the depth and the riches of the wisdom and knowledge of You, oh God! How unsearchable are Your judgments and paths beyond tracing! Who has been Your counselor? Who has ever given to You, that You should repay him? For from You and through You and to You are all things. To You be the glory forever! Amen.

References for All Israel Will Be Saved

1. Romans 11:26

2. 2 Kings 13:2; 14:24; & 15:9, 18, 24, & 28

3. Psalm 106:34-43

4. 1 Kings 11:7-8

5. 2 Chronicles 7:14

6. Romans 9:6

    Romans 2:28-29

7. Luke 16:19-31

8. John 10:26

9. Romans 11:4-5

10. Job 38:2-5

11. James 2:23

12. Revelation 5:9

13. Galatians 3:6-9

    Galatians 6:14-16

14. Revelation 2:27

    Revelation 12:5

    Revelation 19:15

Point of Truth: All Israel will be saved!

Practical Application: Am I part of spiritual Israel, and is there fruit in my life by which the Spirit confirms this? What might that fruit be?

ACKNOWLEDGEMENTS

I would like to express my sincere appreciation to the following individuals that have assisted me in this effort. First to Jerrell Payton, who diligently read and critiqued each devotion and carefully and sometimes painfully helped with scriptural accuracy. Then to Kay Owens, who was my first reader/editor and patiently helped and encouraged me that there was some "good stuff" in there. Then to Brian Everett, one of my pastors, as he also critiqued but more than that encouraged me to persevere in the publishing process. Also, Donna Ferrier, my professional editor/layout designer and also encourager. To my niece, Brooke Woodard, who encouraged me from the perspective of a young reader and did the final edit and critique. And most of all, my wife Cecilia who read, listened, critiqued and patiently encouraged this effort. To all of you a heart felt thank you is due.

Even beyond all of these is Jesus, a friend, savior, creator, giver of life, our very breath and being. To Him be all the glory and honor forever. Amen

Printed in the United States
By Bookmasters